The
Promise
of
Things

The Promise *of* Things

•

Ruth Quibell

MELBOURNE
UNIVERSITY
PRESS

MELBOURNE UNIVERSITY PRESS
An imprint of Melbourne University Publishing Limited
Level 1, 715 Swanston Street, Carlton, Victoria 3053, Australia
mup-info@unimelb.edu.au
www.mup.com.au

First published 2016
Text © Ruth Quibell, 2016
Design and typography © Melbourne University Publishing Limited, 2016

Text design and typesetting by Megan Ellis
Cover design by Mary Callahan
Printed by in China by Toppan Leefung Printing Ltd

National Library of Australia Cataloguing-in-Publication entry

Quibell, Ruth, author.

The promise of things/Ruth Quibell.

9780522868791 (paperback)
9780522870695 (ebook)

Personal belongings—Psychological aspects.
Transitional objects (Psychology)
Attachment behavior.

155.91

For Damon, Nikos and Sophia

Contents

Did you ever see a woman more absorbed in physical objects?
If one looks for her interests, her affections, her desires, one will
find them not lying coiled up in her head but stuck on to the
garden, the meals, the furniture, the hot-water bottle...
Writer Gerald Brenan's dismissal of artist Dora Carrington

Matisse's Armchair

One can feel the need to gather one's thoughts before an armchair …
it is the tender admiration we lend to a familiar object that gives the
object sufficient interest to receive a heart's overflowing.
Matisse's letter to his friend Louis Aragon

The poet Louis Aragon, a close friend of Matisse's, once
wondered whether there wasn't more variety and expression in the
armchairs Matisse painted than in the women.
J.A. Isaak, *Feminism and Contemporary Art*

Yet Another Chair

One day in the spring of 1942, the French artist Henri
Matisse went on one of his trips into town. It might have
been his daily constitutional, insisted upon by Lydia, his
assistant, nurse and muse. He strolled into an antique
shop and there it was, in 'varnished silver, like enamel'—a
striking eighteenth-century baroque chair. 'I have finally
found the object I have wanted for a year,' Matisse wrote
to Louis Aragon. 'When I saw it … I was completely
bowled over by it. It is splendid, I am smitten. With this
chair I shall slowly leap up for the summer.'

As cheering as Matisse's unabashed enthusiasm for
this object is, this was no small achievement in the circumstances. Matisse had spent the last year slowly recovering

from near-death. The chair was part of his stake in the future; his willingness to actively seize a second chance at life.

What was so special about this chair? Even to today's eyes, the rocaille armchair is quite extraordinary to look at. It's a most impractical-looking chair, resembling an open clam, straddled with arabesque flourishes for arms. There are dragon-like faces where the arms meet the seat, and even its squat little legs have an elegance to them. This is not a simple chair for sitting in—it is meant to be looked at. It's easy to be intrigued by its curious combination of strangeness and obvious chairness.

Given the circumstances, though, there were plenty of reasons why Matisse should not have been buying the chair. France was not in a good way, with the north under military occupation. While Matisse was living in Nice, away from the fighting, everyone he knew was touched by it. His daughter was at risk helping the resistance. His son was briefly conscripted, and Matisse was missing his beloved grandson, Claude, who had been sent to live in safety in America. Matisse himself was a seriously ill and increasingly frail man, estranged from his wife. He was, according to biographer Alastair Sooke, bleakly fatalistic about the war and the future of France. 'And now, my dear Pierre, what do you think of the collective madness that is ravaging both the Old World and the new one?' he wrote to his son in 1941. 'Do you feel, as I do, that there is something foredoomed about it, and that the whole world is bent on destruction?'

Why, then, when he felt such foreboding about the state of the world, was he so excited to find an old chair? Surely he knew that no furniture, however intriguing and exotic, would change the basic facts of his existence. More than this, he had no straightforward need for it: Matisse already had a goodly assortment. 'There were Voltaires [chairs with a high scrolled back],' writes journalist Marie-France Boyer, 'neo-Renaissance chairs in studded wood and leather, high-backed chairs covered in damask.' Only months before he'd acquired another favourite: 'the low red and white striped Louis XV bergère,' which, according to Boyer, had 'large well stuffed cushions and [was] trimmed with sophisticated piping'. Why did he want yet another chair?

Promises, Promises

Matisse was, seemingly, doing what so many of us do when our world turns to crap: we go window-shopping, or buy something to distract us or lift our mood. In this strand of thinking, the object is the promise of something beyond itself. For some, it might be a hit of happiness or joy from close proximity to beauty or novelty. For others, it might be the confidence, social standing or admiration that comes from possessing an expensive or widely coveted object, such as a rare painting, a powerful car or luxurious fabric. In each case, having the object can shift us up a notch emotionally or socially, in a way we do not believe we could achieve without it, even if the glow is only temporary.

The word commonly used to describe this tacit expectation that possessions will transform or satisfy us is 'materialism'. In ordinary usage, though, materialistic people are often described as having weak characters: they are portrayed as covetous, greedy, possessive and undisciplined. It is for this reason that many of us are quick to disclaim our attachments to possessions. Yet, material consumption remains common, sustained by the implicit belief that the goods we own will improve us and our lives, even in the face of evidence to the contrary. Georges Perec, in his novel *Things*, gives a sense of how the pursuit of new possessions works. 'Everything was new,' Perec writes of the couple central to his novel:

> Their sensibilities, their tastes and their position propelled them towards things they had never known. They paid attention to the way others dressed; they noticed the furniture, the knick-knacks and the ties displayed in shop windows; they mused on estate agents' advertisements ... Nothing, ever, had equipped them for such new concerns. They discovered them enthusiastically, with a kind of freshness, and were bemused by having spent so long in ignorance. They felt no surprise, or almost none, at the fact that they thought about almost nothing else.

It is not necessarily the objects themselves that are the problem, but the assumptions that guide their pursuit. Critics of materialistic values argue that the hungry acquisition of things is individually destructive and founded upon a socially pathological ideology. Journalist George Monbiot, writing in *The Guardian*, describes materialism as a 'general social affliction' based on a 'dreadful mistake we are making allowing ourselves to believe that having more money and more stuff enhances our wellbeing'. This type of materialism depends upon us believing that human life is compensated, transformed or improved by the ownership of more and better goods.

Implicit in this is the sense that we are in some way incomplete and lacking. Psychologist Mihaly Csikszentmihalyi argues that materialism is so appealing because the solidity of objects offers what our mortal bodies and minds inherently lack. 'Our addiction to materialism,' he explains, 'is in large part due to a paradoxical need to transform the precariousness of consciousness into the solidity of things.' Similarly, as our human bodies are 'not large, beautiful, or permanent enough to satisfy our sense of self' we seek out ways to extend their power, reach and expression through objects. Moreover, as philosopher Crispin Sartwell speculates, new and novel objects and experiences help to reset and re-energise our perception, especially when we tire of the world around us. 'It is a sad and necessary truth about people,' he argues, 'that the things we experience often become commonplace.'

Driven by inherent lack and need for refreshment, there can be no natural cut-off point beyond which all our material needs are met. While we might run up against the reality of financial constraints, even these are no limit to wanting more, and can be transcended with the availability of easy credit. 'If consumption were indeed tied to the realm of needs,' argues sociologist Jean Baudrillard, 'some sort of progress towards satisfaction would presumably occur. We know very well, however, that nothing of the kind happens: people simply want to consume more and more.'

The push and pull of the material world is something many, myself included, struggle with—the Country Road clothes of my teens, the glazed pottery bowls of my twenties, the storage containers of my late thirties. While the practices suggested in popular decluttering books regularly pepper small talk, understanding this push and pull of things requires more than either a practical quick fix or its dismissal as a trivial First World issue. When we already have enough things to meet our needs, what else keeps us seeking out more?

This is not just a rhetorical question to goad us into thinking. There do seem to be real differences among people in how much they need to consume and how attached they are to the objects they own. Those who place a strong value on material goods as indicators of achievement and status are the perfect complement to the capitalist system of production, providing it with buyers with unending, voracious appetites that can never be satisfied. Without them, 'peak stuff' would most likely have been reached long ago. 'Materialism,' as George Monbiot explains, 'forces us into comparison with the possessions of others ... There is no end to it. If you have four Rolexes while another has five, you are a Rolex short of contentment.' For this reason, researchers have dubbed this strand of materialism 'terminal materialism'.

Yet, material acquisitions aren't wholly motivated by 'keeping up with the Joneses', conspicuous consumption, or other strains of invidious comparison to peers. Consumer researcher Marsha Richins and colleagues suspect that people who are highly materialistic have a far 'greater desire to consume than other people'. That is, they not only have heightened interest in, or sensitivity to, the qualities of objects, they also rely on them more. Richins suggests that this underlying difference might be expressed as a desire for more things possibly because materialistic people extract more meaning from possessions, or alternatively lean on objects to provide the meaning in their lives. Certainly, empirical research by Csikszentmihalyi and his colleague Eugene Rochberg-Halton in *The Meaning of Things* found that highly materialistic, emotionally cooler, families seem to have fewer strong and close relationships that provide alternative sources of meaning, value and self-esteem.

The irony here, though, is that while highly materialistic people are heavily involved in the acquisition of things, they don't appear to attach deeply to them, or not for long. Their investment is focused on the acquisition side of the ownership equation and often does not endure over time. They anticipate that object ownership will transform their lives, yet their attachments are typically shallow and short-term. Richins, and her colleagues Kim McKeage and Debbie Najjar, found that 'materialists experience stronger negative feelings after acquisition than do consumers low in materialism'. This phenomena is again well illustrated in Georges Perec's novel *Things*. As all the objects Perec's characters have enthusiastically collected begin to mount up, they lose their lustre. Perec writes, 'indoors it all began to collapse under the heaps of objects, of furniture, books, plates, papers, empty bottles. A war of attrition began from which they would never emerge victorious.'

In an increasingly materialistic culture, this is not only the experience of hoarders, but is becoming a familiar pattern for people in their ordinary lives. Like Perec's characters, we're struggling to keep on top of the things we've bought. Beyond blithe indifference or cynical acceptance, how might we do things differently? How can we respond to the failure of materialism's promise?

7

A Bulimia of Things

'Downsizing', 'purging', 'editing' are all buzzword cures for getting rid of material excess. These practices are often central to the ethos of advocates of the simple life and minimalists, variously conceived along a spectrum from those who do a regular spring-clean to those who opt for a scorched earth destruction of everything they own. The performance of British artist Michael Landy falls at the latter end of the spectrum. He, quite literally, made a radical break with all he owned.

Landy's purge was not in the pursuit of a simpler, less materialistic life for himself. It was for art. He called his 2001 art performance *Break Down* an 'examination of consumerism'. It entailed first cataloguing the 7227 objects he owned, then destroying them. He fed them along a conveyor belt, where workers specifically employed for the task smashed, cut up, shredded and in other ways pulled apart every object. From Landy's own art to a Savile Row jacket, from his father's coat to personal notebooks and letters, everything was pulped. *Break Down* was a brutal separation of an owner from his things in the most transparent and visceral of ways. There was no concealing what was being done. No slow drip-feed of unwanted clothes to the op shop. No passing on of toys to younger relatives. Nothing but patient, methodical destruction. The image that remains in my mind from watching the performance on YouTube is of stuffing being pulled from a teddy bear.

Landy saw his project as a questioning of consumerism and revealing how we end up with so much. 'It's trying to ask,' he told art historian Julian Stallabrass in an interview before the performance of *Break Down*, 'what is it that makes consumerism the strongest ideology of our time? It's as much an open question as an attack.' Art critic Sebastian Smee saw Landy's 'systematic purge' as 'euphorically liberating'. For Smee, the destruction severed the sentimentality that insidiously adheres itself to the ordinary things we own. 'How brilliant,' Smee writes, 'how hilariously theatrical and self-assertive, to catalogue them all and pulverise them in front of an audience of tens of thousands.' In Landy's act, Smee sees an age-old liberation founded on destruction: of what has come before, of who we once were.

Another perspective is that such extensive discarding has become almost normal, even if we hide it from ourselves—as I do in the bag I keep in readiness for op-shop donations. We have to be ready to throw away if we are to consume more; we must set aside what consumer researchers call our 'enduring involvement' with things. This entails a certain degree of deliberate ignorance or forgetting of the consequences. 'We have to believe,' as writer Andrew O'Hagan insightfully puts it in his essay in the *London Review of Books*, 'that the litter of commodities melts into air, just as we do, or else we would have to live very differently in the world ... We don't admit it, but the idea of absence is a comfort to the present, for if nothing is away then everything is a deposit.'

Was Landy's destructive performance an assertion of himself—a breaking free from the sentimental hold of the things he owned? Did the destruction of all that was tangibly material liberate his mind from the hold of materialism? Landy had spent three years documenting and preparing himself for the performance, and considerable time to rationalise the surrender of the things he owned. Still, the impact of destroying these objects had a deeper existential impact than he anticipated. When he was interviewed nine years later, by *The Independent* newspaper, Landy described the unexpected psychological and physical impact. 'Witnessing your stuff being destroyed in front of 50 000 complete strangers is bizarre. People turned up who I hadn't seen for years. It felt like I was attending my own funeral and I became obsessed with the thought that I was witnessing my own death.' His life, in his words, came to 'a big full stop' after his public purge. While successfully revealing the enormity of the collections, and the mundane nature of much of what we keep, the performance left him with nothing—a gap that wasn't necessarily filled by the task of shopping to replace all the things that he'd lost. As an answer to materialism, wholesale purging might better be seen as a briefly cathartic but inarticulate scream, rather than a liberation.

Sensations as Guides

Perhaps, then, we ought to discard more carefully, paying more attention to how we feel about our possessions? While order and rational planning are the central goals of many decluttering guides, feeling is at the heart of Marie Kondo's bestselling manual *The Life-Changing Magic of Tidying Up: The Japanese Art of Decluttering and Organizing* and its follow-up *Spark Joy*. Kondo's advice is to identify what is 'truly precious' to you and discard anything that doesn't bring you joy. It is an appealingly simple prescription. 'I can tell by my client's expression,' she writes, 'the way they hold the item, the gleam in their eyes when they touch it, the speed with which they decide. Their response is clearly different for things they like and things they are not sure of.' (In my experience, though, it is far less clear-cut.)

Kondo uses the feeling of joy to guide uncomplicated, almost mindless action in dealing with possessions. And this has struck a chord with her many fans living in wealthy countries during this time of material abundance. Her admirers range from celebrities to economists, with her books quickly selling over five million copies worldwide. The 'magic' of this quick, intuitive response is a circuit-breaker for those who find themselves unable to rationalise their belongings, stuck in indecision, sentimentality or fear. Instead, the notion of 'sparking joy' allows us to dispense with things without the burden of conscious effort or reason—to not worry about anything else, such as the responsibility of disposing of things. It is a 'magic' of immediacy that one publisher, Susan Bolotin, described in *The Wall Street Journal* as 'almost beyond imagination'. It promises a life-changing clean slate from which to start again, and this time get it right. 'Once you learn to choose your belongings properly,' Kondo writes, 'you will be left with only the amount that fits into the space you own.'

Kondo has given us an evocative method to put into practice. Holding the object, for instance, removes it from the visual world—often occupied by the bloodless images of advertising—and re-engages our tactile sense, and allows the object to actively contribute to how we feel. 'To describe the perception of affect or emotion we commonly use the word "feeling",' writes psychoanalyst Christopher Bollas. 'This has connotations of a physical sense. Just as our eyes see the visual world, we feel the emotional world: we sense emotional states in ourselves and others.' Holding the object focuses our attention, potentially allowing it to be more than something we recognise, but something we perceive. Perception, as Csikszentmihalyi and Rochberg-Halton point out, 'occurs when we experience a thing and realize its own inherent character. It might be a very ordinary object … The point is that the object imposes certain qualities on the viewer that create new insights'.

The practice of holding each object and feeling the emotion associated with it is central to Kondo's method; it is reportedly a very effective technique. But is quick, decontextualised 'joy' all that we need our objects for? Is a simple, immediate assessment of happiness in the moment enough? Writer Adele Chapin found that Kondo's method entrenched a 'materialistic urge', where she 'just kept wanting to discard things and acquire more joy-sparking things … that I didn't expect when I embarked on tidying'. This is akin to the experience of the eighteenth-century French philosopher Denis Diderot when he was given a luxurious scarlet dressing-gown. The gift gave him pleasure, possibly even what Kondo calls 'joy', but it soon went awry. He threw away his old dressing-gown, only to find that his furniture, his books, his shelves and even his chairs now looked shabby in comparison to the new robe. As with Chapin, it triggered a process of finding replacements. 'In the end,' writes sociologist Juliet Schor in her essay 'Learning Diderot's Lesson: Stopping the Upward Creep of Desire', 'Diderot found himself seated uncomfortably in the stylish formality of his new surroundings, regretting the work of this "imperious scarlet robe [that] forced everything else to conform to its own elegant tone".'

12

Diderot's experience reveals not only the potentially burdensome consequences of material upgrading, but also what might be lost in the process: the unnoticed contributions of familiar things. Marsha Richins and Peter Bloch, in research published thirty years ago, suggest that objects will have different ownership trajectories, from those that are based on 'enduring involvement' which is 'stable over time', to those with only a 'situational involvement' that quickly declines. A focus on 'joy' seems to tip the balance towards keeping the new, situational things that may capture our attention in the short term, but serve us poorly over time. Feelings, by their very nature, are fleeting.

And we might want to look deeper and more critically at what this 'joy' is that is sparked, or that we think we long for. The wish of one of Kondo's clients was for a home 'as tidy as a hotel suite'. Yet this wish is for, as *Slate*'s Laura Miller points out, 'the featureless existence of a model in an advertisement, with a weird eternal quality, like limbo'. In this vision of controlled and timeless space, all the work of life is contained and erased from view, alongside the march of time. But if this is what it takes to get out of the muddle of excess, what kind of people are we? What Kondo calls the 'KonMari Method' strikes me as a very effective technique, but one that gives up on what we ought to possess—our own agency and power—in the pursuit of a simple, static happiness that is of dubious long-term value. Our lives, if they are worthwhile and full, are surely more complicated than this, and objects can play more complex and fraught roles in them. While there is the obvious joy of using something that works well, or being surrounded by

13

beauty, Kondo's prescription underplays the complexity and broader emotional range of a life: the swings from joy, to bittersweet loss in memory, to hope in the future.

The pursuit of easy affect like 'joy', detached from the rest of life, might even be at the core of our problematic relationship to things, and the materialistic impulse. As *Affluenza* authors and social commentators Clive Hamilton and Richard Denniss put it, 'the problem is not consumption itself: the problem is our *attachment* to consumption, the way we invest our hopes, our goals and our sense of self in the things we buy and own. The problem is not so much that we consume but that we consume for the wrong reasons.' Or, put more plainly by US academic James Twitchell: 'Getting and spending has been the most passionate, and often the most imaginative, endeavour of modern life.' Materialistic consumer culture is not just a way of living, but has become for many the 'reason for living'.

If we accept, as Hamilton and Denniss argue, that we've been consuming the 'wrong' way, or that we've been expending our creative energies at the mall, as Twitchell contends, then what might an alternative, imaginative life with things look like? The wartime shopping of Henri Matisse provides one example.

A Material Conversation

Matisse wasn't trying to escape his mortality by buying yet another chair. He knew the 'eternal footman' was hard on his heels. 'I watch myself changing rapidly,' he wrote, 'hair and beard growing whiter, features more gaunt, neck scrawnier.' A short time after he wrote this,

his cancer diagnosis, surgery, serious infection and a pulmonary embolism left him in no doubt. He was, as his biographer Hilary Spurling notes, a realist, fond of saying: 'It's no good heading for the grave with your eyes shut.' He knew there was no running away from his body's failure. Still, he asked his doctors for three extra years 'in order to bring my work to conclusion'. He called these extra years his second life, and as always his work was at the centre of it.

But he did not create out of nothing. He needed his faithful objects, collected over a lifetime, from his 'noble rags' of embroidery bought cheaply from street stalls in his student days, to a new chair or two bought in his seventies from an antique shop. Each had their role to play in his lifelong artistic project. They were actors equal to any human model in what writer Marie-France Boyer calls 'Matisse's uninterrupted conversation with his familiar things … they represented an unavoidable need for Matisse. Without them he couldn't paint.' With them, he was free to invent, following his own instinct, sensibility and feelings.

While Matisse added to his collection over time, Diderot's aspirational upgrading of possessions was not for him. Descended from weavers, he developed a strong aesthetic streak, and began collecting scraps of embroidery and tapestry while still a poor student. Spurling describes him as using textiles as a 'strategic ally' in his art. 'He stoutly defended the decorative, non-naturalistic element in painting, and he made luxury—in the old democratic weavers' definition, "something more precious than wealth, within everybody's reach"—a key concept in his personal system of aesthetics.'

15

While we do not know how Matisse chose most of these objects, he most likely responded spontaneously to them, as he did the piece of fabric he saw in a shop window from a bus. But he didn't expect the objects to necessarily offer up immediately all that they had to offer. For that, he put in sustained work by habitually posing and rearranging the objects in still lifes, such as he did with his favourite silver coffee pot. This enduring regard for the object was crucial for Matisse, as he emphasised in his 1947 essay on the importance of the 'profound feeling of the artist before the object which he has chosen, on which his attention is focused, and the spirit of which he has penetrated'. Making the 'mute material world come to life', as writer Rebecca Solnit describes the role of the artist, takes the work of sustained consciousness, rather than fickle expectation. In Matisse's case, this labour of attention lasted more than four decades.

Matisse still occasionally refreshed his perception, in the manner that Crispin Sartwell describes, by adding something new. Matisse wanted, and in many ways needed, his beautiful rocaille chair. But he never expected it was going to solve his health problems. And it was never just a distraction from his imminent demise. He sought inspiration for his life's work—a project that was as consistent as the objects he surrounded himself with. The rocaille chair's curious ornamentation found its way on to canvas: in mustard and olive paint in his 1946 painting *The Rocaille Armchair*, and in black brushstroke outline in *Interior in Yellow and Blue* in the same year. Matisse wasn't chasing a temporary high, but a muse for which he had 'profound feeling', with which new shapes, lights and sensations could be created.

Matisse's Armchair

While Matisse was an artist with specific interests and concerns, his example suggests the hidden or less than obvious rewards of a discerning long-term attachment to these objects. On this issue, Rebecca Solnit makes a useful and vital distinction. 'By *materialistic* we usually mean one who engages in craving, hoarding, collecting, accumulating with an eye to stockpiling wealth or status,' she writes. 'There might be another kind of materialism that is simply a deep pleasure in materials, in the gleam of water as well as silver, the sparkle of dew as well as diamonds.' There is a relationship between matter and materialism, but it need not be in one direction. Matisse's example reveals that it is possible to seek out and be deeply attached to things, to attend to and appreciate them, without necessarily engaging in destructive materialism, or using them as contingent crutches of transformation, only to abandon them at the first sign of their failing to fulfil our expectations. We do ourselves and our possessions a disservice when we extend the problems of consumer culture and materialism uncritically to all the things we possess. On the contrary, we have what these objects will never have: the capacity to think, feel and reflect with honesty on our lives, hopes and goals, and the roles that objects can play in them. And that, I strongly suspect, might mean putting in the work of thoughtful attention to those things that speak to our own life as a whole, rather than just reducing them to joy or rubble.

The Edwardian Wardrobe

Does there exist a single dreamer of words who does not respond to the word wardrobe?
Gaston Bachelard, *The Poetics of Space*

The Container

'Forty cubic metres' reads the removalist's quote. It will take a large truck, several men and many hours to move us—a small family, a couple with two young children. To pick up all our worldly goods, drive them a little over a kilometre down the road, and unload them again at the new house.

Forty. The number sounds enormous. One cubic metre for each year of my life; ten cubic metres for each member of my family. 'Ten', yes, that sounds better, possibly, almost reasonable. Not outrageous like 'forty' does. The removalist, a seasoned expert, reassures me that my family's possessions are a good five cubic metres less than their average move of forty-five cubic metres. And this, in turn, is only a fraction of those hoarders who've kept *everything* from birth. Such hoards regularly peak at ninety to one hundred cubic metres for just one person. Yet I am not off the hook. Professional honesty, I suspect, prevents the removalist from leaving me with a wrong impression: '*But* you do have a *lot* of books.'

Even with the books already packed, I know this move is a tipping point in relation to my things. I not only feel that I have too much, but also that I am stifled, restricted by the responsibility. And many of these objects are simply not worth the effort of packing and unpacking. Moving is often the test of attachment to our possessions. Do they matter enough to pack, lift, shift (or pay someone else to do so) to our next home?

Forty cubic metres. I turn that number over in my head, trying to imagine it as a real space, like an empty Rubik's cube. I begin to mentally fill it with our household goods: the dinner table we sit around every day and its assortment of chairs; the four essential work desks; the functional whitegoods; the four tall bookcases. Real life Tetris. These neat oblongs and cubes are relatively simple mental geometries, as are the 100-plus boxes of books, already packed in the wine cartons conscientiously amassed on each trip to the supermarket.

It isn't the big things that undo me. It is all the miscellaneous, scrappy stuff that interrupts my calm intellectual packing. The unboxed plastic Christmas tree, for instance, with its disobedient branches that refuse to contract, resists and evades these abstract plans, as does the collection of 'just-in-case' paperwork. Most of all, though, I think it is my children's toys that loom as the biggest challenge. They will, no doubt, become box upon box of brightly coloured parental weakness and grandparental indulgence. (I imagine future archeologists speculating our civilisation was built of plastic blocks and worshipped plastic ponies.) When I think of these toys, a mild panic sets in. With moving day rapidly approaching, I walk around the house, looking in drawers and cupboards, and realise just how many things I have still not mentally accounted for or, I have to admit, completely forgotten exist. There is so much unruly stuff still to deal with. I want to call it 'junk' and be done with it. But such an outright dismissal would be dishonest, a lazy generalisation that forgets what these things have done for me, and I for them.

This is the point at which I want to turn my back, up and leave. To disown it all with a slam of the front door because that would save the mental effort, and release me from the running clock's demand. If only I could discard it all as swiftly and determinedly as the liquidambar tree does its leaves every autumn. But I am not a tree and, what's more, this stuff is not going to decompose like leaves, to disappear into dust. I'm reminded of this when I look at my daughter's plastic pony collection, scattered under her bed, and see the blue pony with the pale pink mane from my girlhood. If this stuff will endure, then it is also my responsibility to work my way through it, to use my judgement to sort and sift, and, as the saying goes, 'dispose of it thoughtfully'.

First things first, as I put this responsibility to one side, I have to decide: *What can go?* I walk around the house, plastic bag in hand, scanning surfaces and walls for things I can give away, pass on to the school fete or take to the local op shop. When I reach the bedroom, a candidate stands out: my Edwardian wardrobe. An opportunity to significantly lighten the load in one stroke.

The Obvious Candidate

Tall, with gleaming panelled wood, and a central mirrored door, my Edwardian pine wardrobe is an old friend. We share history. It was my first grown-up purchase when I started working almost twenty years ago. I paid $525. I know this because I kept its neat handwritten price tag from the antique shop. I had never spent so much on furniture and, in all likelihood, never will again.

For what is essentially an oblong box, the wardrobe looks imposing. Over six feet tall, at the bottom is a deep drawer with brass handles that I've always (in an arcane family habit) called a blanket box, even though I keep shoes inside. On either side of the door is the obligatory, yet understated, carved panelling for a piece of this age and style. Along the top edge is a completely superfluous piece of ornate carving. It obviously is out of place. It most likely belongs to another piece of furniture altogether, like a sideboard. The fact that the wardrobe wears it as a crown owes more to the ingenuity of a backyard restorer than the original design, but for some reason this no longer bothers me.

This pastiche, in fact, seems part of its old-world charm of faded grandeur and craftsmanship that evokes another era. It brings something of a ramshackle seaside guesthouse feel to our neat 1950s brick unit in the 'burbs. I know this conjuring is not of the past as it was, but an ideal imagining of how it might have been. It was these romantic evocations of the past that first sold this tall cupboard and its eccentricities to me, rather than any real need to hang up and store the clothes that I rarely ironed. Back then, with only me to think about, functional considerations came far lower down the list.

The wardrobe's glowing, down-at-heel grand exterior is, however, a beautiful lie. A trick of the eye worked by the mirror's reflection. Open the door, and the illusion is instantly shattered. There is no other world to be found behind the mirrored door; no snow-laden forest hidden behind winter coats. It looks more like an austere garden shed, or a tea chest. And it is small. Like a reverse Tardis, it is smaller on the inside: pokey, dark and far, far too small.

Inside, there are a handful of functional, tarnished brass hooks—a reminder of how few clothes people once used to own. 'In 1930,' observes *Forbes* contributor Emma Johnson, 'the average woman owned nine outfits. Today that figure is 30 outfits—one for every day of the month.' In Britain, according to *Stuffocation* author James Wallman, the situation is similar, with the average woman apparently buying fifty-nine pieces of clothing each year.

This old wardrobe could not cope with this amount of clothing. It strains under housing just *my* clothes, yet it once would have been more than adequate for a *couple*, perhaps even a family. It was not made for these days of cheap, abundant chain-store clothing—$2 and $4 t-shirts that cost less than a cup of coffee.

At some stage, someone has sought to bring the wardrobe into the late twentieth century by adding a central hanging rail. (Again, this was a frugal DIY job, made out of what looks like an old wooden broom handle.) It's a serviceable solution creating more hanging space, but it is a tight fit. Clothes have to be squished to hang at a 45-degree angle for the door to close. As a result, the central door hinge has now weakened and the brass doorhandle has fallen off. It is far from perfect.

The most obvious flaw—the one I never even considered when I bought it—is its size. While it isn't overly heavy, it is unwieldy. It has always been a two-person job to move it, although at a pinch, I can slide it around on the floorboards. I tell myself that if I were more sensible, more utilitarian and less sentimental, I would've ditched this robe long ago. The amount I could've saved on moving costs, both professional and personal, would've bought more than a few pairs of the decent boots I so enjoy wearing (and wearing out).

But I haven't. In fact, most of the time I don't even notice these defects. Why?

Despite its hulking mass, the wardrobe is, like most of the objects we own, part of the invisible backdrop to intimate, domestic life. Sociologists Tony Kearon and Rebecca Leach, in their exploration of the experience of being burgled, call this invisibility of things the 'habitus of comfort'. In our familiar everyday environments our possessions lose their 'thingliness'. They lose what marks them out as separate and alien from us. Through familiarity their existence becomes an unthought extension of ourselves in intimate space.

The invisible second naturedness of objects, however, is not forever. Any changes that disturb our material habitat, or our relation to it, create the potential for thingliness to return, and with it the grounds for reassessment, separation, succession and disposal.

The wardrobe has survived eleven house moves. From the home I grew up in, to one bungalow, to three flats (with stairs), four houses in the suburbs, and one unit. With each move, some of my possessions have become open questions, their future up for grabs. This move was no different. The wisdom of keeping the wardrobe was again called into question, although this time it was me doing the questioning. The scales were tipping towards getting rid of it. It had become, as gerontologist David Ekerdt puts it, a candidate for dispossession. But *only* a candidate.

Active Dispossession

'It will give us trouble no doubt,' wrote the nineteenth-century socialist, artist and designer William Morris, 'all this care for our possessions'. Morris, who was writing about the broader civilising goals of art, gives voice to a familiar, yet rarely acknowledged, sentiment: possessions require effort. Cleaning, protecting, storing and all the other ways we care for them, are work. Most of the time, when we are in fair health, this routine care requires little more than regular energy. As we age, though, or as more responsibility for housework falls on the shoulders of one person, this upkeep can become a drain. The things themselves may also start to show their age, looking shabby or worn or threatening to fall apart. 'Ageing is a worn chair,' writes historical geographer David Lowenthal in *The Past is a Foreign Country*, '... it is a house with sagging eaves, flaking paint, furnishings faded by time and use.'

The artist Vanessa Bell, in a letter to her daughter Angelica in the year before she died, described this burden.

'Everything in the house is simply falling to pieces,' Bell wrote in her March 1960 letter, 'and after a bit it rather gets on one's nerves ... The chairs seem to be going to fall to pieces in a day or two ... I am becoming aware of ghosts.'

As we change, so too often does the value we place on our possessions and, with this shift in perspective, our willingness to do the work of keeping them.

However, just sitting an object on the scales does not necessarily mean that we actually complete the task of weighing up its virtues, let alone ditching it if it is found to be less than worthwhile. Most people first try giving it away or selling it, with throwing out the final option. Giving an object away has twofold benefits. In finding someone who values it as we do, we rescue it at the same time as passing on responsibility. Selling means that we can recover some of the sunk cost, which allows us to feel better about its loss, while also transforming it: the personal thing is returned to being a sellable commodity. Throwing it out is usually the action of last resort.

I consider all three options for the wardrobe. Yes, I could give it to my mother—she doesn't have built-in wardrobes and extra storage might be handy for her spare room. The wardrobe would be at home among her antiques, and she isn't moving any time soon. As I deliberate, she even offers to have it delivered. But I know this is her kindness speaking, and this feels far too much like passing the buck—adding a burden when she is busy stripping back, reducing her material load. And she is already surrounded by other people's furniture: caretaker of inherited things passed down to her.

The Edwardian Wardrobe

Of course I could pay to store it until … until when? Paid storage would solve the problem in the short term, but I would be spending money I could put to other ends. My indecision would cost me.

Instead, I make a few calls to the dwindling number of nearby antique and second-hand dealers—a once established shopping strip of quaint black-and-gold lettered shops, now gradually being replaced by development. A sole dealer calls me back to confirm what I suspect: it is the wrong sort of wardrobe—no one wants these ones anymore, not when they can buy cheap, new flat-pack furniture assembled with an Allen key. The world of things has changed in the last twenty years.

The wardrobe has no resale value. There will be no recovering of my original investment in the piece—what economists call the 'sunk costs'. That money was spent almost two decades ago, and the wardrobe has given good value at less than $30 per year. This should make me feel better, but it doesn't. As psychologist Barry Schwartz explains it in *The Paradox of Choice*, his book exploring the downsides to a culture of abundance, this is because 'we hate losses'—especially ones that stick around as reminders of this fact. But I suspect that the flatness I feel is more than this.

Short of selling the wardrobe for parts, or finding another sucker like me who would love it—and these options would take time I did not have—I could give it to charity. That is, if one would come and take it within the time I still had. Failing that, I could leave it on the curb for council collection as hard rubbish. But I didn't have the heart to do either. So what to do?

Useful or Beautiful

I return to William Morris's evocative ideas about things. Today he is best known for his ornate wallpaper and tile designs, but Morris had a far larger canvas in mind when he wrote and delivered his socially engaged public lectures, *Hopes and Fears for Art*, in the late nineteenth century. In his 1880 address on the beauty of life to the Birmingham Society of Arts and School of Design, he canvassed a wide range of topics. From the importance of satisfying work for the labouring classes, to the need for education for all, from railing against the screechiness of advertising, to rallying for the enforcement of the Smoke Act against the coal-burning industrialists who continued to flout it ('these gentlemen, many of whom buy pictures and profess to care about art, burn a great deal of coal').

Unifying his speech was a central theme: the importance of beauty for civilisation, and how fragile this is in the face of industry, haste and the quest for status and superfluous luxuries. The builders of houses, he argued, are likely to assume

> that we want the pretence of a thing rather than the thing itself; that we want a show of petty luxury if we are unrich, a show of insulting stupidity if we are rich: and they are quite clear that as a rule we want to get something that shall look as if it cost twice as much as it really did.

Morris believed this status-seeking at the lowest cost, on the one hand, and industry expediency, on the other, threatened to overwhelm those reformers who wanted fundamental change. His advice was to begin on a smaller, individual scale. He advocated simplicity that begins at home.

Morris's 'golden rule' was simple (although I imagine him bellowing it as a command to his audience). 'HAVE NOTHING IN YOUR HOUSES,' he capitalised for emphasis, 'WHICH YOU DO NOT KNOW TO BE USEFUL OR BELIEVE TO BE BEAUTIFUL.' Morris wanted us to think about the significance of how our homes look and work, and how they might be simplified, stripped of the unnecessary. He wanted us to be what psychologist Barry Schwartz describes as intentional 'choosers', rather than just 'pickers' who quickly 'grab this or that and hope for the best'.

Morris wasn't writing for these times of Western countries' material abundance, but his ideas are perhaps more relevant than ever. Today his rule of thumb is widely cited by contemporary designers and declutterers alike. It has an intuitive, commonsense appeal. It is a call for action. It cuts through status anxiety and the expectations of others in a single stroke. It is an easy maxim to keep in mind. I once complained of the baby-clutter clouding my home and brain, and a colleague, with the clarity of a spotless office, replied with Morris's words of advice. The phrase lodged in my brain for future use.

Morris was nothing short of clear. He even went so far as to list the necessary ingredients for a late-nineteenth-century sitting room: a bookcase 'with a great many books in it', moveable chairs, a bench, a cupboard with drawers, a vase or two of flowers, 'real works of art' such as pictures or engravings, or if you cannot afford them, wallpaper or hangings: 'the wall itself must be ornamented with some beautiful and restful pattern'. While I have the requisite bookcase, chairs and flowers, he, unfortunately, makes no mention of bedrooms and wardrobes.

Sitting in a twee Melbourne tearoom, a week away from moving, I am surrounded by one of Morris's green swirly wallpapers. In every direction, wall space is covered with acanthus leaves, accentuated by black woodwork. I do not know if Morris would have endorsed its visual busyness. I do not find it very restful or beautiful. To my eyes it is cluttered and claustrophobia-inducing. It is a struggle to believe that this could be the creative fruits of a leading proponent of simplicity. For now, though, I try to put these doubts aside and return to my wardrobe problem in light of Morris's golden rule.

Useful

Morris is not a lone wolf in his praise of usefulness. 'Everyday utility,' says gerontologist David Ekerdt, 'tops any list of possession motives, lay or scholarly.' We keep those things that are useful to us now, or *might* be in the future. You can see how easily slipping in the word 'might' tips the scales in favour of keeping things you know are long past their use-by date—the backup can opener, for example, that doesn't quite work, but doesn't take up much space in the back of a drawer. As this suggests, usefulness is a relative, not an absolute, standard. Useful, we might ask, for what? For whom? At what time?

My wardrobe is *in* use. Every day I store and sometimes hide my too-difficult clothes from me. I don't want to see their ragtag assemblage of chain-store basics, hand-me-downs, op-shop bargains, and what this might say about me. I know from my occasional reading of home magazines and the seemingly innocuous annual Ikea catalogue that there is a higher standard out there—wardrobe equivalents of bells and whistles. These wardrobe planning systems even promise to solve the subjective problem of feeling you have 'nothing to wear' with 'smart interior fittings [to] help organise your clothes so you see exactly what you have'.

By contrast, my old wardrobe does the clothes storage job at a far lower standard. It is dark and cramped. The clothes I rarely iron usually hang awkwardly and crumpled. I could be less dishevelled, more polished. Built-ins and specially designed robes offer genuine, superior affordances, such as pull-out railings, dividers, dedicated sock drawers, good lighting. My art teacher tells me his walk-in even has its own lighting (less helpful when he forgets to turn it off and is awoken by the light glowing behind the closed door, like something from an alien abduction or horror film).

The evaluation seems cut and dried: my wardrobe is a relic. As David Ekerdt points out, 'things have meaning not just in themselves but also in relation to others'. Before I knew better, my wardrobe was a pain to use, but its awkwardness was normal. And yet, I am suspicious of these better options, because not only am I imperfect, but also because I'm not sure what the attainment of ideal usefulness would look like or feel like. Usefulness, on its own, is not a good guide here. There is another question, as psychologist Barry Schwartz reminds us: 'the first choice you must make is between the goal of choosing the absolute best and the goal of choosing something that is good enough'.

Schwartz's broader argument in *The Paradox of Choice* is that we live in a time when choices have been multiplied, and when making the *best* choice has been elevated to something akin to a moral responsibility. Morris's maxim, on first blush, seems to sit quite nicely in the marketplace of choice, especially among those with a life-simplifying product to sell. In the mind of those people who Schwartz terms 'maximisers', Morris's praise of 'useful' becomes the golden standard of utility: 'you seek and accept only the best'.

I'd like to think that there are situations where I seek the best—my endocrinologist's treatment advice swiftly comes to mind—but Schwartz points out that when it comes to consumption and ownership of goods, maximising is a recipe for endless searching, dissatisfaction and time-wasting—or all three. Schwartz's alternative is to be a 'satisficer'. Like the slightly imperfect 'good enough' mother, which my maternal and child health nurses regularly invoked, the satisficer isn't someone who settles for mediocrity. Satisficers are not bereft of standards and criteria, but the world isn't at stake if she makes a mistake: if the baby gets a bottle, or the mother buys the slightly wrong shade of navy. A satisficer is doing well enough, but isn't continually dissatisfied.

I had been aware of my wardrobe's limits, but it wasn't until I had to move it that I took another harsher, more critical look at it. Now, in light of Schwartz's guidance, I look at it and myself again. Who do I want to be?

Perfectly Imperfect

My husband, a 'carry-on luggage only' kind of person, has already packed up his sparsely populated built-in wardrobe. He makes it look easy, this translation of possessions back to their thingliness. Like an overzealous gardener, he has swiftly and severely pruned his wardrobe of its contents, reducing them to little more than a small suitcase and a laundry basket. He appears to relish the opportunity to get rid of the things that have served him: the poorly fitting jeans, the slobby jumpers. He does so without much overt hesitation or sentiment. He does not seem to be worried about loss, but appears assured that the prune will yield new growth.

I am not so decisive, light and nimble. In addition to the weight of the wardrobe is all the clothing stuffed within. The 'clothes sense', as Virginia Woolf dubbed it, is a mysterious one. (Woolf promised her diary she would write more about it, but aside from the fiction *Orlando*, she never wrote an essay on it beyond the notes in her diary.) My own wardrobe and its contents, assembled on an enduringly low budget, is the site of connection, or mismatch, between my inner and outer identity—who I think I am and how others see me. The wardrobe clearly has other uses than the obvious one of storage and organisation. It is my last remaining refuge of privacy in a life shared with my husband and our children; children who go through everything, from jewellery boxes to underwear drawers, and yet who know that the wardrobe is off limits. It is where I hide their birthday parents. It is a safe container of these conflicting goals and emotions, and as

I consider them, I realise that I'm not quite ready to cast it aside.

While I can see these personal uses, what of its restrictions? Its limits?

They have not disappeared, but I now see them differently. 'Within this utter constriction,' writes philosopher Crispin Sartwell of his experience learning to play the blues on a simple harmonica, 'I am perfectly free, I am not trying to play correctly or to play a song the way it *should* be played' (my emphasis). This complements one of the crucial points made by Barry Schwartz. There might be objective standards of excellence, but these are always experienced subjectively. And here is another crucial difference between maximisers and satisficers of life. Satisficers might feel better about their less-than-perfect choices than maximisers do about their objectively better ones.

The pursuit of perfection can be unduly psychologically taxing. The small size of my wardrobe is not perfect, but it adds a helpful external layer of discipline—it both limits the number of my clothing choices and makes me more conscious of when I am making them. Whenever my wardrobe gets too full, it is a spur to reflection: about what I need, who I am, who my audiences are (and how much their good opinion matters), and what I value. Does being slightly crumpled matter? Asking these questions is a counterbalance to my reticence to make decisions on what to keep or let go.

Working with these constraints imposed by the wardrobe has focused me on having a 'good enough' small range of clothes that works for me. And this has been liberating. I have a reliable core of favourite shapes, colours and textures, rather than chasing every trend. They anchor getting dressed each day. Less choice, somewhat counter-intuitively, is more satisfying and requires less time and effort. I don't feel as if quite so much is at stake as when I had the wardrobe *and* a built-in.

Living with the wardrobe's physical limitations is a prod to improvise, both in how I store clothes and how I wear them. The dark corners that are difficult to access, for instance, are the perfect spots for storing out-of-season clothes in those magical shrinking vacuum bags. The back of the mirrored door, just the spot for hanging scarves, in easy range to coordinate or contrast with faithful jackets. The battle scars from wire hangers provide the impulse to exchange them for the smaller, pretty padded satin ones, which are much better for my clothes in the long term.

Of course, there is no necessary causation here. The wardrobe has afforded constraints, and I've chosen to view working within these constraints as beneficial. 'A chooser,' as Barry Schwartz points out, 'makes decisions in a way that reflects awareness of what a given choice means about him or her as a person.' He continues, 'a chooser is thoughtful enough to conclude that perhaps none of the available alternatives are satisfactory, and that if he or she wants the right alternative, he or she might have to create it'. On balance, I hope I am a chooser.

Beautiful

Years before I acquired the wardrobe, I met its visual counterpart in the beautiful interiors paintings and drawings of modernist Australian artist Grace Cossington

Smith. While Cossington Smith is better known for her café scenes with red chairs or the cityscapes with Sydney's unfinished Harbour Bridge in full view, it is the feeling of her later, 1955, *Interior with Wardrobe Mirror* that has remained in my memory. The painting has the hint of a bedroom reflected in the wardrobe's mirror, an oriental rug on the floor. It has the simple, vivid intimacy of Van Gogh's colourful *Bedroom in Arles*. Yet Cossington Smith's work seems to glow vibrantly, shining with the morning sun. And this was her intention. She wrote in 1965:,

> My chief interest, I think, has always been colour, but not flat crude colour, it must be colour within colour, it has to shine; light must be in it, it is no good having heavy, dead colour … The room is in my own home here, and the sunlight did not come in a definite way but the whole room seemed to be full of light, which is what I want to do more than the actual sunlight. I feel that even the shadows are subdued light and they must have light in them as well as the light parts.

At its best on a sunny day (and especially *on* a sunny day), this is what my wardrobe does. It has come with me, after all. The removalists, delivering it in my absence, have positioned it in the new house adjacent to the bedroom window. The mirror absorbs all the available winter sun and reflects it back into the room. It's as if another window has been added and, together with its warm wood, it creates an aura of relaxed domesticity. An ordinary suburban bedroom becomes a Grace Cossington

Smith painting. And this makes me feel good. I feel at home here.

Psychologist Sam Gosling in *Snoop: What Your Stuff Says About You* points out that particular objects can make us feel a certain way. They are 'feeling regulators', objects we use to improve or sustain our mood. In the context of getting dressed, if I already feel good, the clothes I wear matter less. Less is at stake. I can more easily settle for 'good enough', and get on with my day. (Of course, feelings are highly subjective things. For my husband, who has lugged the wardrobe's dead weight from house to house for six of the eleven moves, it is no mood enhancer—aesthetic merits matter little relative to the burden of heavy lifting.)

After the emotional turmoil over whether to keep or discard it, I'm now relieved to have kept the wardrobe. The anxiety I felt over deciding its fate has dissipated. How? The work of psychologist Daniel Kahneman and his colleagues on 'peak-end' experience offers some insight here. He suggests that how we remember an experience is shaped not by the facts, or the pain or pleasure it causes, but by our memory and feelings about a given event at two key moments: how it feels at its peak (good or bad) and its end. Had I rid myself of the wardrobe at its negative peak—when it felt so burdensome I didn't know how to resolve it—I doubt I'd be having my feeling of Grace Cossington Smith-type beauty. But having kept it, and reached the positive peak at the end, my judgement has shifted. Of course, I was right to keep it, I think.

Twenty years after I first handed over what seemed like an enormous amount of money to buy it, my wardrobe and I are both a little the worse for wear. Yet, I've learned more about my relationship to objects, particularly clothes, from this odd partnership than I suspect I ever would have from pursuing some mythical 'ideal' closet. I know what the choice to keep it has cost and given me, and I'm aware of my limits—how I might act differently in different circumstances. I've learned that, for now, the ideal working wardrobe for me is distinctive, old and small. It might be heavy and cumbersome, but it removes some of the unnecessary burden of choosing what to wear each day, sparking a little creativity, and helps to put me in, or to sustain, a good mood or improve a bad one. Little wonder we're still old friends. Perhaps I'm just easily satisfied. Today I fixed its broken brass handle, installed a fancy new scarf rack—a Morris-inspired concession to improving its usefulness—and gave it a good polish.

The Ithaka Stone

We must rediscover for ourselves the mystery of comfort, for without
it, our dwellings will indeed be machines instead of homes.
Witold Rybczynski, *Home: A Short History of an Idea*

The Consolation

As I lay in the dark, listening to the moonlight mutterings
of the old hospital, I was trying to hold myself together,
solid, firm, substantial. Trying to hold onto *this* world—
to not give in to the recurring sensation that my blood was
boiling like a shaken can of Fanta. In my palm, I cradled a
smooth, egg-shaped stone. Sleep came and went, but I did
not let the stone go.

The trip to the emergency room on New Year's Day
was supposed to be routine— 'Probably nothing', said
the Irish locum, before adding his customary, 'God bless'.
I knew I was sick, and had been inconveniently bedrid-
den over Christmas and New Year's Eve, but suspected
influenza. I remained stoic, optimistic, patient; even as

the emergency department hour turned from one to three; even as my husband took our tired children home to bed. *I'll get a taxi home later*, I thought blithely.

But as that night drew on, I unravelled as the flustered registrar asked yet another of her hushed queries about my (non-existent) drug history. By the time the tired, stripe-shirted specialist arrived and flatly delivered his diagnosis and prognosis—unreal statistical probabilities, like a child's Choose Your Own Adventure—I was too sick to comprehend them. But I knew the plot had changed. A little later, when the uncontrollable vomiting began, the straw wall around my emotions collapsed. I was no longer in charge.

That first harrowing night, my husband returned in the wee hours, and held my hand. We talked about what would happen if tomorrow never came for me. It did, but the next morning I was quarantined, isolated, alone. We didn't know the risks for him and the children. The nurses, who entered only when they had to, wore gloves, some face masks. The cleaner, attired in yellow plastic, didn't stop to exchange pleasantries but hastily finished her work and got out.

My husband dashed home to check on the children, arrange a roster of carers, and to collect hospital essentials: PJs and books. Even in his haste, he paused by my desk to bring me something perfectly useless, something with no obvious place in that sterile room. A mere oversized pebble, a stone plucked from a Mediterranean beach a long way from home. He wasn't sure why he brought it. He just thought I'd like to have it, to hold it.

A week before I had been overwhelmed by the tactile stimulation of motherhood and domesticity: changing nappies, washing up dishes. A month before I had been busy, in the self-imposed isolation of working to deadline. Now, in this strange place, in a hollowed-out and depleted body that no longer felt like my own, I wanted nothing more than to hold and be held—to feel connected to that ordinary world. As I cradled the stone in my palm I was struck by the sense that this inanimate object—a simple holiday keepsake—was holding me, rather than the other way around.

Masters and Servants

It is tempting to end thinking about the stone here, and just be grateful for this anchor of familiarity. It would be easy to conclude that the stone made me feel normal and safe because it evoked the security and simplicity of my pre-illness life. In this view, it was not the stone at all, but what it represented that comforted me. But to do this is to conclude too quickly, too easily, to forget the intimacy of inert things and how regularly, sometimes unconsciously, they provide us with tactile, embodied comforts.

Every day, we live intimately and unthinkingly among inanimate things, engaging with them not just abstractly or visually, but in an embodied fashion. 'Each morning,' for instance, as neurologist and author of *The Hand* Frank R. Wilson explains, 'begins with a ritual dash through our own private obstacle course—objects to be opened or closed, lifted or pushed, twisted or turned, pulled, twiddled or tied … The hands move so ably over this terrain that we think nothing of the accomplishment.'

Some time after, I returned from hospital, into the new normality of post-illness recovery, the volume of everyday

41

life was turned up. I was paying attention to things I had previously taken for granted. One morning, as I washed the breakfast bowls, and my young daughter began to get restless in her highchair, I handed her a freshly washed willow pattern teacup. At scarcely a year old, this was the first non-baby china cup she'd held in her chubby hands. (This might seem rather careless, but my mother-in-law had given us twenty-seven mass-produced ones.)

Her assertions of 'Out—Now!' were silenced. She turned the cup upside down, tasted the sides and bottom, felt the patterns on the sides with her fingers, then looked at them carefully, before turning it upright and putting her chubby fist through the handle, and settling on the everyday, ordinary way she'd seen me hold it. As I said the word 'cup' over and over again, I realised I'd just witnessed what I'd long forgotten: that we learn *from* the world, gathering and putting all the sensory information together about an object in an embodied way. The object isn't a passive player in this education. It doesn't just mean whatever we decide it will; it pushes back.

Now my daughter is five, she no longer needs to pay as much attention to the cup, only to ensuring a safe voyage of the liquid within it to her lips. By the time she is an adult, she will have mastered this too—she'll pick up her tea or coffee to drink without even noticing the cup or worrying about spilling its contents. Her body will remember what to do. Through mastery, the cup will become a ready-to-hand extension of her body. When this happens, she will become blithe in her relationship to many objects, as most adults do, and they will become less visible, less worthy of her attention.

We usually think nothing of this contact, in part because we have mastered these complicated manoeuvres, but also because the things have become part of commonplace experiences too trivial to notice. We forget not only what is close at hand, but also what we have mastered. 'Once acquired,' as sociologist Tim Dant points out, 'we often do not notice these objects until they break or are commented on by someone else'.

We spend most of our days this way, oblivious to the company of inanimate things. It is little surprise then that we assume them to be our docile servants, with us their masters. Unlike our contact with people, our encounters with possessions are assumed to be one way. When I put my pen down, I can expect to find it in the same place. Similarly, it is *I* who buys, and disposes, of things at *my* whim. This suggests that objects can only have the power and meanings *we* give to them. And yet, on my nights of lonely West Ward tears I was no longer so certain of my dominance and mastery. I was intrigued and wanted to understand how the stone itself had comforted me. How can inanimate objects do this?

The Stone Itself

In the hospital, I had instinctively picked up the stone from the trolley, nesting it in one hand and then the other. Immediately, holding it calmed me. The deep wobbly feeling, of unseen terror, eased. My chest relaxed and expanded. I could breathe deeply. At first, it was cool to touch, but quickly warmed like skin. It felt like the weight of a hand resting in mine, like my son's hand when he was a toddler ready to cross the street—a hand I could no longer hold in my alien yellow skin.

In my mind, the stone is pure, brilliant white, as it had been on that sunny beach when I had walked over hundreds of such smooth stones. In fact, when I look at it now I see that it is barely white at all. It is marbled with blue veins, with discolouration from the oils left behind by being habitually held—by me and by those others who, unthinkingly, cannot resist the urge to pick it up from my desk.

Asymmetrical but balanced, like a chicken egg but without any sense of fragility or weakness. It is solid, it weighs down my palm. I do not feel in any danger of dropping it. I now know its irregular edges and weight so well that I suspect I could, blindfolded, tell it apart from any other.

The stone fills my palm, stimulating the touch-sensitive nerve fibres scattered there. My fingertips are by far more sensitive—the human hand has around 17 000 touch-sensitive nerve fibres, according to John M. Henshaw, author of *A Tour of the Senses*, and they are more densely distributed on our fingertips. Searching over the stone's smooth, curved edges, they quickly find the tactile equivalents of light and shade: textures and hidden indentations.

Even now, several years after my illness, quietly holding the stone still comforts me, and makes me feel more fully alive. If this comfort is a purely physiological response, how does it become meaningful?

Embodied Perception

It is tempting to think of the stone as a set of observable properties that add up to a stone. The stone is its shape *plus* its colour *plus* its texture *plus* its weight, and all this together *adds* up to the mental idea of the stone itself. This atomised accounting of properties is, according to philosopher Maurice Merleau-Ponty, the dominant mode of thinking about objects. However, for Merleau-Ponty, the object is a 'unified identity' that is more than the sum of its observable parts.

An object does not have a meaning that springs pure from its itemised qualities, but from their intermingled unity and how we experience this unity. This is a two-way relationship between the object and its user (or the one who experiences it). The object's qualities can only be understood, argues Merleau-Ponty, 'in light of the dialogue between me as an embodied subject and the external object which bears this quality'. Honey, in Merleau-Ponty's example, is sweet and sticky, but we cannot know this abstractly. We learn it fully when our hands are made sticky, when we are honeyed. Like the stone in my palm, it pushes back. Honey reveals this relationship more obviously than other objects do, but it is not an exception. 'Our relationship with things is not a distant one,' writes Merleau-Ponty, 'each speaks to our body and to the way we live. They are clothed in human characteristics (whether docile, soft, hostile or resistant) and conversely they dwell within us as emblems of forms of life we either love or hate. Humanity is invested in the things of the world and these are invested in it.'

This intertwining of people and objects is explored further by Thalma Lobel, a psychology professor of embodied cognition at the University of Tel Aviv and author of *Sensation: The New Science of Physical Intelligence*. Lobel explores how our tactile perception of an object's texture and weight can, unconsciously, scaffold our actions and experiences, and influence how we act. 'Touching rough, smooth, hard, or soft objects,' for instance, 'influences how rough or smooth, hard or soft we perceive a situation to be and how hard or soft our behavior is'. There is, according to Lobel, a complex interplay between textures, metaphors and how we conceptualise the world.

Sometimes, this correspondence is deceptively obvious. Weight, for example, appears to influence judgements of seriousness. In one study Lobel describes, participants holding a heavier clipboard gave more serious weight to social issues. In another study, students holding weightier clipboards estimated various currencies higher than those holding clipboards that were half the weight. Unconsciously, weight appeared to add substance. Did the literal weight of the stone make such a direct difference to me? Did the smoothness of its surfaces take the rough edge off my struggles? In the face of sharp physical decline, did it help me to hang on? These are suggestive ideas to entertain, although I have no way to know this for certain—I cannot trust my illness-addled recollections. This was, though, how it seemed: as though the stone anchored me, making me feel more substantial, less ephemeral, and stopping my nightmares from taking flight.

Holding and Being Held

Holding and being held are common, soothing responses to distress. 'Without human touch,' writes nature advocate

The Ithaka Stone

Richard Louv in his bestselling *Last Child in the Woods*, 'infant primates die; adult primates with touch deficits become more aggressive.' Babies are cuddled, yet as we grow up we cannot be assured of receiving physical comfort from others when we need it. Increasing numbers of us live alone, or through screen-mediated lives. It is easy to forget the consolation of things, but, as sociologist Tim Dant reminds us, 'our contact with objects is continuous and intimate in comparison with our contact with people'. We do not lose touch.

In *An Anthropologist on Mars*, the well-known writer and physician Oliver Sacks describes the 'hug' or 'squeeze' machine invented by Temple Grandin, an academic with autism. Grandin developed the machine to satisfy her need to be held. As a child, she had experienced contradictory impulses of longing to be held, hugged and cuddled but also being terrified and overwhelmed by human contact. She still craved the pleasure and peace of being held, and began to dream of a magic machine that could hug her while she remained in control. In response to this need, she invented her 'squeeze' machine. The V-shaped, upholstered 'body-sized trough' is based on a squeeze chute for restraining cattle. Using an industrial compressor, it exerts firm pressure over her body, from her shoulders down to her knees. 'She could not turn to human beings for solace and comfort,' writes Sacks in his fascinating account of his time with Grandin, 'but she could always turn to it.' While Temple Grandin's innovative response to her need for tactile comfort is unusual, turning to objects for solace is commonplace.

The concept of the 'transitional object', as developed by psychiatrist and psychoanalyst Donald W. Winnicott to explain how infants and children use familiar objects to comfort themselves when separated from their carers, is now a commonly accepted idea in child development. Body parts such as thumbs, alongside familiar objects such as dummies, toys and blankets, are often used by infants to self-soothe. Winnicott's idea has gained popular currency, popularised by the Peanuts character Linus with his blanket. My son's 'Woofy' and daughter's 'White Ted' played just such important roles in their imaginary play and bedtime rituals.

Transitional objects, which Winnicott also called 'comfort objects', are often held close to the child's body. Sometimes partly destroyed by love, as sociologist Deborah Lupton observes, these objects are not kept pure but are 'created' or 'customised' by the child. As with Grandin's hug machine, these objects contribute a sense of calm through being held, aiding the child to be soothed in the absence of a carer, while also aiding their development of a separate sense of self from their carer.

Intimate, soothing inanimate companions—Temple Grandin's preference—make sense in the early childhood years, but what of everyone else? In that hospital room, with the noise of the world turned down, unable to touch or be touched, the small white stone in my palm stood in for people. While the circumstances of my illness and hospitalisation were exceptional (one in a hundred, was the specialist's estimate), the comfort of objects is not. In our ordinary, everyday lives, whether we know it or not, we regularly find comfort in, and are comforted by, the objects in our homes.

A Nest of Comforts

'What is comfort?' asks architecture professor and author Witold Rybczynski in *Home: A Short History of an Idea*. It is a simple question that can be answered straightforwardly as only concerning 'human physiology—feeling good'. We know something is comfortable, consoling, because we feel it. We also know comfort by its absence, through feeling uncomfortable.

Yet for Rybczynski, such purely subjective physiological explanations are insufficient. What of the variations in domestic well-being over time and place, and between individuals? The modern idea of comfort, he points out, was once neither commonplace nor widespread, but emerged in rococo France. It then evolved in the relaxed bourgeois domesticity of the eighteenth-century British country house. In its later expression, material comfort was also increasingly viewed as connected to inner psychological states like contentment. 'It is surprising,' he writes,

> how often one comes across the words 'comfort' and 'comfortable' in Jane Austen's novels. She used them in the old sense of support or assistance, but more frequently she intended them to convey a new kind of experience—the sense of contentment brought about by the enjoyment of one's physical surroundings. She described Fanny [Price]'s room [in *Mansfield Park*] as a 'nest of comforts'.

Over time, seeking comfort from and being consoled by material things, physically or psychologically, became a widely accepted cultural idea. This is the domestic well-being of a comfortable home that we now take as given.

Today, it makes sense to think and speak of comfort in our homes, as interiors writer Deborah Needleman does, as something that makes us feel good—it is a domestic atmosphere. Comfort, she argues, makes us feel 'taken care of' and looked after by embracing us 'in the mundane'. Once in our private universe, we can, in clichéd form, close the door on the world, let our hair down, kick off our shoes, or put our slippers on.

The comforts and consolations of particular objects from the homely ensemble can be difficult to unpack beyond a positive reaction to specific things. 'Dullness,' as Witold Rybczynski puts it, 'is not annoying enough to be disturbing, but it is not stimulating either. On the other hand, when we open a door and think, "What a comfortable room," we are reacting positively to something special, or rather to a series of special things.'

Rybczynski suggests we try to richly describe our experiences of comfort. In this way we might discover its, often unconscious, layers, such as its physical, psychological and physiological ones. His example includes the following elements: 'convenience (a handy table), efficiency (a modulated light source), domesticity (a cup of tea), physical ease (deep chairs and cushions), and privacy (reading a book, having a talk)'. All these characteristics together contribute to the atmosphere of interior calm that is part of comfort.

It is noteworthy that this description shares much in common with William Morris's prescription for an ideal sitting room. This does not seem coincidental. Each has paid attention to what the elements offer to our experience. This observation and reflection is the start of figuring out what things might matter to us—an essential part of an intelligent life with things. Most of us, though, in the rush of life, will never get this far.

Comforting Indifference

Writer Richard Louv, who coined the evocative term 'cultural autism' to describe nature deficits, has made a compelling case about the dangers of our children losing primary contact with the natural world. For Louv, the natural world is a primal necessity—the world of human artefacts are of lesser value, especially the dead-end electronic tools many of us now live through. We are, Louv argues, in danger of losing the capacity to 'see, feel, taste, hear or smell for ourselves'.

One consequence of a world that is increasingly mediated through electronic screens is that we use our senses in a narrowed way. While children still respond bodily to bees, falling leaves or bicycles, and walkers and joggers to the rain and flies, they also use their fingertips on a screen. As the mother of a screen-enamoured, game-playing 8-year-old boy, I am sympathetic to Louv's argument, particularly his point about the dangers of losing close personal interaction with the immediate and sensory world.

Another crucial difference is that the natural world is not made with us at its centre. When the natural world is sidelined by electronic battles and passive screen time, for instance, not only are our senses responding to a restricted range of humanly designed stimuli, we also remain at the centre of things. My hospital room was not devoid of useful but indifferent sensory stimulation, but I was at its centre. The stone, however, resisted my touch in the most basic physiological way. It was not malleable, and I had no desire for it to be so. Unlike William Morris's advice, it was neither useful for daily life nor conventionally beautiful, and the absence of these qualities was central to its fundamental appeal. It was not a docile servant, but an ancient thing in itself, indifferent to my human world and its needs and urgencies. It will endure long after I have died. It was the thing that stood apart, indifferent to my feelings. Like Temple Grandin's hug machine, it was devoid of human intimacy, and its demands and rewards. A stone just is.

Epaphus

'Epaphus', writes the Greek writer Nikos Kazantzakis in his fantastic fictionalised autobiography, is 'the god of touch'. Epaphus does not trust what he sees or hears, only what he feels. He 'wants to touch, to grasp man and soil, to feel their warmth mix with his own, feel them become one with him'. Where the others are fickle sky gods, Epaphus is reliable, industrious and earthly. Yet, throughout his life, Kazantzakis was also tempted by Epaphus's spiritual opposite, or nemesis: Buddhism, where 'pain is an illusion, an ephemeral dream that will vanish—you will wake up and it will have scattered. Then you will vanish and the world will vanish with you'.

In that anonymous hospital room of bleach, jarring yellow hazard bags, and existential uncertainty, I wavered between these opposing tendencies. Between the sense of being engulfed by impending doom and threat of losing everything that mattered to me, and the urge to completely withdraw into numbness. I could so easily have discarded the world and ceased to care about anything. It was the stone with no obvious purpose that brought me back to this world. It satisfied my basic need to touch and to feel, and in doing so cut through this utter desperation. The stone made me feel anchored in *this* world. It weighed me down when I know I so easily could have slipped.

The Poäng

Industry which means modernity, seriality, perfection, the run of objects that don't just approximate each other, but are each other. It is standardisation, it's the on and on and on of things in the world.
Edmund de Waal, *The White Road*

A Troublesome Spine

The seating problem must be solved, I realise, and quickly. The sudden onset of sharp pain running down my husband's left arm seems to come out of nowhere. He goes to the doctor, who advises that the symptoms are not to be ignored. This is soon confirmed by a scan. The pain is the result of nerve damage to his upper spine, possibly caused by an unlucky landing in judo class. An eerie intermittent numbness begins in his hand and fingers. The doctor is direct: complete rest for ten weeks, she says, with obvious concern on her face. No lifting anything more than three kilograms. 'But, the baby,' my husband objects, to which she replies, 'Nothing, not even the baby.' Not possible, my husband begins to protest, but the doctor, obviously well versed in dealing with noncompliant patients, does not hold back. This is serious, she states, the risk of paralysis is very real. This is the one thing that reaches the impatient 30-year-old, who until now has been cavalier about the strength and resilience of his still-youthful body. She repeats her instructions, for good measure. Rest. Complete rest. Ten weeks. Heal.

The point forcefully made, he and I and the new baby are left to put these words into practice at home. It sounds so simple. Rest. Good postural habits. Upright, support-ive seating. But exactly how do you support a decade-long computer warrior to achieve this end? This becomes my abiding practical problem to solve. My husband does his part to mindfully sit up all day, trying not to slump or slouch into habits years in the making. But it is physi-cally tiring for him to make such changes even in the short term, let alone for over two months. While visitors ignore or downplay even the idea of paralysis, he and I cannot do the same. Pain and numbness regularly intrude, and in response he becomes mindful of his every move. We are on tenterhooks as never before.

Our home, I realise, is a physiotherapist's nightmare. The plain hardwood kitchen chairs only offer so much sup-port, while the feather-stuffed couch demands slumping. Even lying down in bed is an issue, as lying completely flat brings on the telltale numbness—the reminder of damage hidden behind pale flesh. A body unexpectedly transformed changes our relationships to the objects we live among even more than bringing a baby home. None of our familiar, well-worn furniture can be adapted to meet this singular need for support. I cannot fix my husband's injury, but I can try to find a practical solution. A new solution.

The Poäng

Most people in a similar situation, I imagine, would probably do the same thing. But going out to buy something brand new feels both strange and perfectly normal, as if I were now inhabiting the uncanny reality of TV furniture advertisements. Until this point in our lives together, as a reasonably able-bodied couple with a limited budget, we had been content to build a second-hand life, waiting for the 'right'—affordable and interesting—objects to turn up. Furnishing our home was a kind of open-ended adventure, rather than a dedicated task to quickly tick off and complete. It consisted, accordingly, of one part objects found in antique shops in holiday towns, to two parts things gleaned from hard rubbish collections or hand-me-downs, rather than new things from retail shops. With the exception of bedding and white-goods, only a handful of the things for this home had been bought new. This was at least partly a conscious response to environmental and ethical concerns—concerns that now felt heightened in the presence of a sleepless baby and late nights spent reading *The Guardian*'s environmental pages online. But I also acknowledge that it was an unexamined habit mixed with a suspicion of things that weren't old enough to have stood whatever arbitrary test of time I had in mind. What I hadn't realised was the way this entrenched habit obscured the degree to which these assorted objects actually met our needs. With other priorities competing for my time, and enough bodily leeway to allow for imperfect furniture, I basically hadn't needed to pay close attention to each object's fitness for purpose. Now, though, functionality entered my deliberations as the pre-eminent value, the card to trump all other values.

'I know what can fix this,' I say to my husband, as if the mortal threat occupying his mind and body were merely an administrative muddle in need of better organisation. I load our 3-month-old son into the old white Volvo, rarely driven in months of sleepless nights, drive down the busiest road in town, then along the tram tracks to the big concrete mall. It is opening time, but I won't be here long. I am shopping with one intention: to quickly find and buy a new and cheap chair to solve these new difficulties. The solution, which I have already found in the catalogue, even has a name. It is called the Poäng.

Everywhere and Nowhere

A Poäng is a mass-manufactured armchair from Ikea. Originally created by designer Noboru Nakamura in 1975, it was to be 'an armchair for life'. Intended to be a 'comfortable, durable and attractive chair', but also a cheap one, the chair looks relatively fragile. Unlike many cheap things, though, it is demonstrably durable. Inside the shop, my son and I watch through a clear perspex case as a robotic machine tests the chair, its pneumatic arm hypnotically pressing up and down on the seat, in mimicry of a lifetime's worth of the average adult sitting down and getting back up again. You can trust this chair, the machine seemed to say, and here is the proof.

The Poäng was recently included as one of Ikea's 'famous five' objects, a list of its 'all-time top 5 products', according to stylist and blogger Chris Carroll. This list also includes a popular sofa, a lampshade, a familiar small coffee table and a bookcase with adjustable shelves. The bookcase, which like the Poäng is known to many by its name, is called a Billy. It is Ikea's most popular product, according to UK *Telegraph* feature writer Harry Wallop. This is not an empty claim to popularity. Writing in 2012, Wallop noted that over half a million Billy bookcases had sold worldwide in less than two months. (I confess, we have two second-hand Billies: one containing a collection of graphic novels in the kitchen, and another that shelves the book overflow in our garage.)

While Ikea has not released information on how many Poäng chairs have been made and sold over the world in four decades of production, it is fair to say that they seem ubiquitous. American writer Meghan Daum, in her autobiography *Life Would Be Perfect If I Lived in That House*, aptly captures how recognisable the Poäng is to many people. It 'was a nice chair, if an utterly common-place one in the post-IKEA world', she writes, 'the neighbours came over and said, "Oh, the Poäng!"' I have seen this chair on design blogs, like *Apartment Therapy* and *Design* Sponge*, in several neighbours' houses, in offices and op shops, and occasionally left out on the nature strip for hard rubbish collection. My children even recognised a grandmother sitting in this chair in one of their story-books, *Eddie's Kitchen* by English writer and illustrator Sarah Garland.

This chair is part of the enduring wallpaper of con-temporary life. It is what anthropologist Janet Hoskins, drawing on the ideas of French sociologist Violette Morin, might call a 'protocol object', an object that is 'everywhere and nowhere, marking not a personal expe-rience but a purchasing opportunity'. But what type of purchasing opportunity is this serially produced object, its appearance an obvious nod to the modernist design sensibility? What opportunity does it hold out to the purchaser?

Function

The Poäng has an exposed skeleton of 'layer-glued bent beech'. Its wooden curves and dips echo the elegance of the human spine—I only truly appreciated the strange beauty of our inner architecture when I saw my unborn son's spine on an ultrasound. My hope is that the Poäng's outer spine will give my husband's damaged one the support it needs. It promises to do this by following and mimicking the curves of his body. This is how it feels to me as I test out sitting in it in the showroom. But unlike my husband's damaged vertebrae, my hope is that the Poäng will not harbour any surprises.

Stripped of any ornamentation and superfluous padding, the Poäng is not an ordinary armchair. It exposes what the traditional stuffed armchair usually hides. It consists of a sparse wooden frame with a thin neutral cushion. It looks skeletal by comparison with its more traditional counterpart, such as the heavy leather Chesterfield club chair. Not surprisingly, it weighs far less too. At less than nine kilograms, it is around the same weight as a 9-month-old baby boy; a tenth of the weight of the Chesterfield. As I load its flat-packed parts into the trolley, this is no small consideration. For the foreseeable future, I know I'll be the one carting it around.

Stylistically, the Poäng's restrained use of materials is firmly in the modernist design tradition. The Poäng's bentwood frame, with its veneered legs that double as armrests, bears more than a passing family resemblance to the modernist chairs of the early twentieth century. These include the 1930s springy designs of Finnish architect Alvar Aalto's '31' armchair and '39' chaise longue, and Marcel Breuer's 1936 curved plywood Isokon 'Short Chair', although it should be noted that Breuer's use of wood was a concession to the manufacturer's perception of British taste.

The Poäng, like these stylistic forerunners, looks somewhat vulnerable. It has none of the reassuring bulk that gave the hulking lounge chairs of my '80s childhood their impression of enduring solidity. It is unlikely that my son will grow up to use the Poäng as a launching pad for lounge-room gymnastics when my back is turned, as I used to do on our lounge chairs as a child. (Another part of my new mother brain is, having confronted the stark reality of bodily injury, quietly relieved to have eliminated this risk in advance.) Nor will I have to worry too much about spilled drinks and other damage to its limited, washable upholstery. In fact, the Poäng's only ornamentation—if you can call it that—is found in the two striking cantilevered wooden legs that curve upwards to form the armrests and down along the floor to form the legs.

It is a chair reduced to its essential functionality. While it can be relaxed in when used in the proper way, it is almost impossible to comfortably lounge, slump or slouch in it. And this functional discipline is for our own good—for the health of our spines—or so it would seem.

Transformation

Back home again, I put the pieces of the new chair together on the lounge-room floor by following the diagrams.

It takes me less than half an hour and comes together with Lego-like simplicity. This is a rather hollow achievement, especially compared to the challenge of actually building something from basic materials. But even this limited participation in the chair's creation makes me feel better about buying something new. It gives me a degree of grudging respect for the distant production process that can guarantee such an outcome, over and over again. And it leaves me with a warmth I hadn't expected. I feel a slither of fondness towards this chair, even though it is completely indistinguishable from any other bearing the same name. Researchers have even given a name to this positive feeling that often goes along with building flat-pack furniture: 'the Ikea-effect'.

The Poäng's presence in my home, much to my surprise, changed my attitude to it. Its existence seemed to suddenly shift my expectations of what an object could offer, and with this, the relationship between me and the other, far older objects within the house. But how exactly?

For French sociologist Jean Baudrillard, in his book *The System of Objects*, the object is always transforming or mediating our relationships to the world in some way. A car, for instance, transforms our relationships to space and time. A mirror changes our relationship to light and, more often than not, our own appearance. A radio burbling in the background shifts our relationship to silence and sound, to morning birdsong and traffic. For each of these dynamic, reflective or noisy objects, the overt transformations they bring are easily identified and recognised. But what exactly does a mass-made and static object, such as the Poäng, transform?

The Poäng

The most obvious fact about the Poäng was how clearly it did not fit in. I was under no illusion that it would, but the extent of its outsider status is noteworthy. Aesthetically, it was out of time: too new, too minimalist, too perfect, too functional, too unmistakably Ikea. But there was also something strangely reassuring about its novelty compared to the weight of the old things. Its very newness seemed progressive, as if it were unburdened by any historical assumptions, and unshackled from the weight of my personal history. Meghan Daum makes a similar observation of what her husband's Poäng brought into her home: 'something about having it in the house was gratifying'. She observes, 'The lines were clean and minimal, the exact inverse of the house itself.'

At first, this response makes sense. The often-stated design philosophy of modernism is that it is a rational response to human needs for function, explicitly unimpeded by the weight of tradition and sentiment. The ideal of functionality ostensibly becomes the chief determining criteria of the shape and appearance of objects. It has often been reduced to a mantra: form follows function. It isn't so much that instrumental use is at the top of the hierarchy of values, it is that there is no longer any hierarchy. Form and function are the only values that matter. With criteria such as these uppermost, designers were liberated from having to follow traditional styles. No longer did chairs, tables, cupboards, need to look a certain way, with surfaces covered with superfluous decoration, to serve their fundamental purpose. Form did not need to be hidden under chair skirts, or obscured by floral flourishes such as carved acanthus leaves.

While the resulting designs are often aesthetically minimalist, other claims were also smuggled in about their purity, honesty and cleanliness. 'Scandinavian design of the 1930s,' writes architectural historian Steven Parissien in *Interiors: The Home Since 1700,* 'dealt with themes popular in the postwar West: practicality, flexibility, convenience, hygiene, dignity (if not humour) and ethical responsibility.' Modernism also became a code for aesthetic stylishness and social progressiveness, even though neither of these associations was the necessary or automatic consequence of objects made in a functional form.

In the eyes of the proponents of modernism, traditional designs were associated with a conservative sentimentality, or put more crudely, were caricatured as favoured by an older generation unwilling or unable to move with the times. Functional furniture, by contrast, was seen as the furniture of the progressive future. 'As the machine age progresses to simplify our lives,' a mid-twentieth-century furniture catalogue for Douglas Snelling chairs states, 'we should accept its advantages intelligently and not clamour for imitations of past centuries.' Instead of the handcrafted objects of an earlier age, the catalogue explicitly championed the technology of the emerging machine age. This 'undisguised product of modern machinery' was 'scientifically designed and constructed to give the greatest amount of comfort and durability'. These functional chairs might have been unburdened by history, but they were loaded with high expectations of progress.

The Liberation of the New

'What is the implication,' ask researchers Mihaly Csikszentmihalyi and Eugene Rochberg-Halton, 'of the fact that only 7 percent of the West German population in 1965 preferred traditional overstuffed furniture, whereas 35 percent preferred modern Scandinavian design'; and of the fact that most—two in every five—chose a contemporary-style coffee pot, rather than an antique-style reproduction? Was it a sign of social and aesthetic rejection, an eager embrace of the new, or something else entirely?

At the same time that the West Germans were embracing Scandinavian design in greater numbers, Jean Baudrillard was describing two dominant systems, or ecologies, of household objects: the traditional and the functional. These two main systems, he contends, reflected, shaped, constrained or liberated how people lived in their homes. The traditional system that was historically associated with the middle-class family in France was, however, giving way to a new system based on functional furniture and more liberated interpersonal relationships.

Traditional middle-class houses, he observes, were based on a hierarchical layout, usually around the needs of the nuclear family, with the assumption of a patriarch at its head. This family structure was reflected not only in the family relationships, but also in the home's fixed layout, and the unchanging, often old and heavy furniture that went with it. As continues in many dwellings today, the traditional home was a private realm, largely separate from society and protected from the outside world, with the relationships of family members reflected in the objects, rituals and routines. It is a system of fixed, authoritative power relations, in a specific geographical place.

But this place-bound and authoritative system was quickly losing ground to an emerging 'functional system'. The functional system of objects promised to liberate the individual from place as much as formal relationships. It was characterised by the flexibility, lightness and agility promoted in open-plan layouts and smaller, convertible spaces, such as flats. In the functional system, the connections between furniture, rituals and routine were negotiable and made 'more supple in their uses', as Baudrillard puts it. The dining table and its formal rituals, for example, were replaced by the informality of the coffee table. Their owners, like the objects themselves, were more relaxed, open, liberal and, importantly, mobile. The functional object is liberated from any other claims, such as those made by the 'moral theatricality of the old furniture'. Within this new system these objects have, as Baudrillard puts it, 'the freedom to function, and ... that is practically the only freedom they have'.

In modernism, the functional system has a socially progressive public face, mirroring in some ways the broader liberating social movements of the twentieth century, from feminism to disability activism, that explicitly advocated a more emancipated, less institutionalised, less hierarchical and gender-rigid world. Yet the link between objects and actions is not this straightforward. What's interesting here isn't so much that systems of objects tend to convey and reflect existing social relationships, but how little we tend to notice these when in close proximity to them.

It wasn't until the Poäng was in my house that I could glimpse some of the values implicit in the Edwardian wardrobe, the mahogany kitchen table, the painted faux-colonial desk. I could see the shadow of the traditional system and its assumptions about solidity, fragility and permanence. Their contrast with the Poäng threw into relief some qualities of weight, texture and colour, especially in the heavy wardrobe, or the delicate desk's curved legs, both of which were, for different reasons, not designed to be moved.

Alongside this, I realised that what I had taken to be purely aesthetic choices were actually loaded with assumptions about place and continuity in the solid objects made to last, rather than be regularly moved or disposed of. These were objects made to endure—objects for what the sociologist Zygmunt Bauman calls 'solid times'. The Poäng suddenly seemed light, but perhaps too light to commit to. While the presence of the traditional system is easy to recognise in hindsight, the more recent functional one exemplified by the Poäng has tended to escape such scrutiny.

67

Ephemeral Times

The function at the heart of modernism is a pledge that these objects have finally got it right; that they are the best for whatever purpose they are designed for; that their form will endure because of this fitness for a specific purpose. The fact that there is a widely recognised canon of such objects and their designers (often architects) is akin to a compact ensuring their continuity. But it is no such guarantee at all. It is probably doomed to fail for several reasons.

As a set of aesthetic principles, modernism has no inherent ethics or morality. Its objects may appear to have

an enduring status as exemplars of progressive design, but
they do not stand outside of power relations. Modernism's
principles, as director of the Design Museum London
Deyan Sudjic, writing in *The Guardian*, puts it, 'could
be put to use by anyone'. Christopher Wilk's modernism exhibition at London's Victoria and Albert Museum,
Modernism: Designing a New World 1914–1939, for
instance, included a lesser-known pavilion sketch by leading modernist Ludwig Mies van der Rohe for the Brussels
Expo of 1934. This was probably an everyday pitch for
work, but the sketch 'for Hitler ... complete with swas-
tika flags and Nazi eagles' reveals the vulnerability of the
modernist movement.

68

Moreover, these designs are just as vulnerable to being
replaced by better forms as the traditional forms they
themselves supplanted. Baudrillard writes that 'it even
happens that a new object will be adequate to its function while at the same time working against it'. Even relatively unchanging objects are subject to this process. In
the well-known Spike Jonze ad for Ikea, a working lamp
is put outside on the curb in the rain because it has been
replaced by a new one. As rain falls on the old lamp, the
voice-over tells us not to feel bad for the lamp as it has no
feelings. The new lamp, the voice claims, is 'much better'.
But better how? This advertisement illustrates one of the
limitations of an appeal to pure functionality to defend
an object in the fickle laboratory of freedom that is late
capitalism.

'Something in design has gone wrong,' writes Deyan
Sudjic, 'when objects don't mature in a way that makes
them more desirable.' Yet functional success or failure, as the Spike Jonze advertisement indicates, doesn't

necessarily play a significant role in the object's devaluing. This is partly a consequence of the interchangeability of mass, serial and cheap objects that means I need not care for or worry about them, in the same way as I do the irreplaceably unique, old or expensive. I am safe in the knowledge that not only can I find something like it, but that I can find an object that is all but indistinguishable. There is nothing special or precious about the Poäng, for instance. If it were broken, I could just as easily replace it. This is why *New Yorker* contributor Lauren Collins writes that 'IKEA has made interiors ephemeral'. But it is not only price that has made such furniture ephemeral. We have accepted a new 'compact' that furniture is not expected to last a lifetime. 'Perhaps we don't want the object to last forever,' suggests *Cheap* author Ellen Ruppel Shell. 'We have grown to expect and even relish the easy birth and early death of objects.'

But this isn't necessarily a compact that has been willingly grasped, ignorant to the wider environmental and economic consequences. Those who reject family heirlooms aren't merely turning their back on what Baudrillard calls the traditional system and embracing the functional one. They are also accepting a system which nudges them to replace, a decision often made in the pursuit of 'progress' and 'function', but these actions might be reluctant or at least more mixed than they first appear. Psychoanalyst Adam Phillips, talking about the constant feed of social media, likens it to 'force-feeding', even if we're complicit in this eating. It is a type of gorging without recognising what this is doing to our appetite. The point might be fruitfully extended to illuminate the urge to have more and new things. 'There is a strange, magical idea,' writes Phillips, 'that you can consume without digesting, that you could eat without swallowing as though there were no process.' In this sense, the liberating relief we feel at having shallow, flexible attachments to functional objects might be understood, at least in part, as preparation to purge, to make way for the next thing. What kind of liberation, then, is to be found in new, cheap, functional furniture?

Liquid Times

Two years after Ikea released the first version of its Poäng—its 'chair for life'—two researchers were asking American families to tell them about their most significant possessions. Household furniture, such as chairs, sofas and tables, was frequently nominated, with 638 different reasons why they were special. The researchers Mihaly Csikszentmihalyi and Eugene Rochberg-Halton concluded in *The Meaning of Things* that household furniture was what made many people feel settled and comfortable at home. In the almost four decades since this study, the stability of our homes and working lives can no longer be taken for granted. As with our objects, enduring stability is, for many, more of a memory than reality.

The chief virtue of our current age, argues Bauman in *Liquid Times*, is not function but flexibility. Flexibility and its buzzword synonyms 'agility' and 'positioning' make claims to energy and optimism, but essentially they come down to being prepared to act, shift and change ourselves swiftly. On this point, Bauman's words best illustrate the shift from the stability of solid times characteristic of the mid-twentieth century, to the liquid times of globalised capitalism in the early twenty-first. 'The virtue proclaimed to serve the individual's interests best is not *conformity* to the rules (which at any rate are few and far between, and often mutually contradictory),' he writes, 'but flexibility: a readiness to change tactics and style at short notice, to abandon commitments and loyalties without regret.'

This momentum beyond our control is part of the 'on and on and on of things in the world', as writer and ceramic artist Edmund de Waal evocatively puts it. This all-encompassing flexibility extends to the material world as well as the domain of an individual's actions and expectations of labour, for instance. It is reflected in the retreat from long-term thinking and stability, as much as it is in the withdrawal of long-term financial and emotional investments in people and places. Its logic enframes how we act, even if it does not wholly determine it.

We can attempt to recognise the functional system, its implicit values, and reflect on the interests it serves, which are unlikely to be completely our own. Importantly, shallow material engagements can be resisted, with the right supporting conditions. Ikea's founder, Ingvar Kamprad, has reportedly used the same Poäng chair for decades. 'I've had it for 32 years. My wife thinks I should get another one because in the meantime the material has got dirty,' the world's fourth-richest man told *The Guardian* in an interview in 2006. 'But technically it's as good as new.' He had no plans to replace or upgrade it. But the wealthy Mr Kamprad is the exception to the rule in more ways than this.

Imperfect Offerings

My Poäng looks exactly like the one in the catalogue. It is just as comfortable and functional as the one I tried out in the showroom. At least, for me, it is. But I learn quickly that it does not work as intended for my injured husband, who is a few inches taller. He tries it over and over again, but cannot get comfortable—the headrest cuts into his neck at precisely the wrong place. (This, I later realise, is not an uncommon complaint made in online reviews of the Poäng.) We concede failure: the chair will not fit the man, and the man cannot adapt to the chair. Instead, the man, to my surprise, quickly abandons the idea that there is a solution 'out there', and creates a make-do solution with an old, heavy chair and a complicated cushion arrangement. The kind of homemade solution we would have once taken for granted.

The purely functional solution I sought has failed. My husband rests and recovers. And I am left with an object I never quite wanted. Of course, the agile thing to do would be to return it to the flow of things. But with flagging energies dissipated by worry and care, I defer the task of disassembling and returning it for another time. That was almost ten years ago. The Poäng is still with us. Age has not wearied it, although it has frayed its cushion.

Was it the Ikea-effect, inertia or a heightened (some might say 'pathological') responsibility for the object that I had bought in a flight from panic? Almost a decade on I cannot confidently say it was any of these things. At some point, perhaps in the midnight hours as I gently rocked my firstborn back to sleep in it, I took to owning the chair as an opportunity to study my responses to it, to a functional object so clearly not of my own choosing. It failed at its original purpose, but so what? I still recoil slightly from its ordinariness, but it offered me a fruitful clash with my own assumptions and habits. And it has become other things beside this: a nursing chair, soothing to rock in, with low arms; a recovery chair during illness, when it seemed to cradle and comfort my frail body; a gaming chair for the baby who is now a Minecraft-playing pre-teen.

The entire system of value seems weighted against keeping the Poäng. I was supposed to use it, and let it go when it had served its function—my purpose. But what limited idea of purpose is this? Not every object needs to be old and solid, or new and disposable. We can choose otherwise. We can live with the clashing interplay between them, and refuse the assumed superiority of one over the other. Ordinary and functional is fine too.

The Velvet Jacket

If an object you now control is bound up in your future plans or in your anticipation of your future self, and it is partly these plans for your own continuity that make you a person, then your personhood depends on the realization of these expectations.
Margaret Radin, *Reinterpreting Property*

Hunter, Collector

'Serendipity.'

'Fortunate happenstance.'

'A pleasant surprise.'

These are the words I probably would have used had someone asked why I was, once again, browsing in an op shop on an early summer's day. Although none of these reasons are quite correct. I wanted luck to shine on me, but I was not there by chance. Like many op-shoppers, I knew from experience that this shop was worth my time looking in. That amid the excess I was likely to find something that would have an impact on my life. I was, I admit, somewhat addicted to the possibility that an op shop presented. I anticipated finding something discarded as worthless and transforming it into something of value for me. And like my fellow treasure hunters that Saturday morning, I had the sense that whatever I was likely to come across was just around the next cluttered aisle.

For close to two decades, op shops have fuelled anticipation and expectation. As I stand looking in their windows, I think: what might I find in here? I suspect others feel something similar about ordinary retail expeditions. Rarely are these types of browsing trips driven by definite need. The role of chance, however, is higher in the op-shop environment. On its shelves and racks, no matter how well organised, there is rarely any certainty of finding exactly what you are looking for, like the correct size shirt, or the number and colour of bowls you need. Even with the increasing standardisation and churn of cheap objects, the search remains much more akin to gambling than normal retail shopping.

This atmosphere of chance overrides the smell of ancient mothballs, the textures of microfibre suiting, and the somewhat disturbing thought that at least some of these objects are dead people's things. Perhaps these things ought to concern me more than they do. But the promise of the serendipitous find is an unusually powerful one. In my case, it is a stubborn search in the face of failure. It is an anticipation that one day I will stray across not just a lucky find, but the one that I have always been looking for: the perfect velvet jacket.

The 'Find'

I run my hands down the racks, quickly, impatiently, searching for something I doubt is here: the distinctive resistance offered by velvet. More precisely, I'm looking for a fitted brown velvet blazer. After almost two decades, browsing in every op shop I pass by, my expectations of success are low. Yet still I keep up the search. It's become something of a quest—my private op-shop challenge.

Today I do not have the luxury of indulging my browser's curiosity. The sounds and smells of the busy shop threaten to wake my week-old baby, resting against my body, from her delicate sleep. As she snuffles on the edge of wakefulness, I chastise myself. Any reasonable person would have waited until she was properly asleep, or never ventured into the shop in the first place. But this search was never a reasonable one. It is about the strangely evocative power of a coveted object.

I am midway through my self-recriminations—'bad mother'—when the unexpected happens. Before my brain has registered it, I have parted the racks and pulled out something made of brown velvet. But it is not just the usual musty, well-worn velvet jacket. It is a perfectly preserved, tailored blazer, despite its vintage and the stench of mothballs. Its brown velvet gleams under the shop's fluorescent lights. It is only $8. Yet, I hesitate—I can't quite take it in. I call to my husband, who responds with an enthusiastic thumbs-up. I go to the counter, pay and then head out into the summer day.

When I get home, after I put my baby down in her basinet, I try on the jacket. And this is when the problem begins. It doesn't quite fit yet—I have just had a baby— but I am confident that it will. That is not the problem. For some reason, I am disappointed with this object that I've coveted for so long. Now, when the op-shop gods have finally smiled upon me, the jacket is only just a jacket, and I am not the person I'd anticipated meeting in the future. A feeling like regret settles in my mind where once there was a spark of hope. Clearly, this is about more than just the jacket. What had I expected possessing this coveted object would do for me?

An Idealised Future

The wish is for something I do not have, and might never have: to be liberated, stylish and chic. This is more modest than the ambitious First-World aspirational longings for status, wealth and social mobility (although it is undoubtedly tinged with them). Longed-for, difficult-to-attain objects, like my jacket, are usually coveted for some time from a distance. Some may be costly or rare, but not always. Some, like my velvet jacket, are just plain difficult to find. This is usually not, argues anthropologist Grant McCracken, the basic wish to possess an object that we do not own. Instead, in our minds, these types of objects 'tell us not [only] who we are' but 'who we wish to be'. It's a simple enough idea: a much-wanted object evokes an ideal future self.

Optimism about finding the desired object becomes intertwined with the hopes we have for our lives. 'The consumer,' writes McCracken, 'looks forward to a life that is, finally, fulfilled, satisfied, replete.' Writer Rebecca Solnit makes a similar point about the perpetual playing house of interior decoration. For Solnit, stage-setting of the home is not just an expression of boredom or triviality, but a fundamental expression of hope—'hope that everything will be alright, that we will be loved, that we will not be alone ... that our lives will be measured, gracious, ordered, coherent, safe'.

In our minds, these sought-after objects can provide a reassuring link between the present world, with all its rough edges and difficulties, and the idealised future we will live in once we possess the object. Perversely, the solidity and tangibility of the object come to stand in for a personal state that is out of reach, while also making it seem possible. Their very thingliness lends our ideals a hint of tangibility, even if these ideals remain dimly acknowledged, fragmented and idiosyncratic. 'Goods,' suggests McCracken, 'have the virtue of suggesting, even demonstrating, this substance, through their own substance.' This is a variety of magical thinking. McCracken calls it the 'peculiar epistemology of common sense', in which the existence of the solid object is used as empirical evidence of our ideal life: the life we want *does* exist, as does this object, even if we do not possess it in the here and now.

Even for those who reject such magical thinking, the object can still powerfully evoke a future self, complete and authentic. A truer version of our self at a future point in time, or in a different set of circumstances, in which we no longer have the burden of deciding who or what we will become. To the question of 'Who will I be?', comes the life-simplifying answer: 'The person with the velvet jacket'. In this, we're relieved of all the complicating freedoms we confront on a daily basis: ambitions, responsibilities to others, and the burden of finding meaning or purpose. The object is the promise of relief from becoming anything other than an owner of an object.

But owning these objects is rarely a stepping stone to living this life. Rather, it often transforms into what

Rebecca Solnit painfully characterises as, in her essay 'Inside Out, or Interior Space (and Interior Decoration)', a form of elaborate procrastination. The dream of possessing the desired object becomes 'the eternally postponed preliminary step to taking up the lives we wish we were living'. Setting the room for the guests who do not arrive.

Safe Choices

The coveted object represents a meaning bundle that combines an emotional quality with specific circumstances. Objects are safe places to park our dreams and fantasies. Through them we can cultivate ideals and aspirations. They can help us to provide tentative answers to the recurring question: 'What should I be doing with my life?'

Coveted objects are the perfect vehicles for projecting ideals onto. Inanimate objects cannot refuse our mental projections. Indeed, the very act of seeking and choosing an object bolsters the belief that we are actually free to shape our selves. Shopping fosters this illusion of choice. 'Here you can believe you control your own destiny,' argues sociologist John Carroll in his book *Ego and Soul: The Modern West in Search of Meaning*. 'Make yourself, transform your life.' And in uncertain times, it can help to believe the illusion that we're in control.

The objects we do choose to buy will not laugh at, or contradict, us. 'It's an embarrassing fact,' writes philosopher Susan Neiman in *Why Grow Up?*, 'that we are often more afraid of embarrassment than a host of other discomforts, but it isn't less true for that.' Objects will not demand us to be more realistic, face facts or focus on outcomes. As symbols, props and reminders, they can help us to cultivate those intimate ambitions that might otherwise shrivel in the face of too much scrutiny.

The potential reward of the evocative object is that it is part of an elaborating conversation with ourselves—a conversation in which we protect fledgling hopes and cultivate goals. But this carries the risk of retreat into private fantasy, where objects become compensations, allowing us to avoid the pain of living. While any coveted object can be a bridge to our imagined other lives, in order to remain a safe repository of our private projections they must remain *just* out of reach. This is why they are usually just beyond what we can afford, in some way unique or rare, or, in my case, extremely difficult to find.

Covetous consumption can invoke the often frag- ile, hopeful fragments of our imagined future lives while also shielding them from the harsh light of reality. The coveting from a distance is crucial. This strategy pro- tects the ideals by removing them to another time, such as a future in which we own a coveted object. With tan- talising things, we protect ourselves from the frustration we would otherwise feel about the gap between our day- dreams and reality.

In my own case, I think this strategy began by acci- dent. The searching for a blazer that might or might not exist became a thingly extension of how life felt to me: contingent. I worked hard and achieved, but I was quickly learning that plans were not the roadmap to certainty. In the search for the jacket, however, contingency could be rebadged as possibility, probability, happy coincidence. 'This is the one,' writes Jenny Diski of her shopping con- sciousness. 'I've found it. It has found me ... I have the garment I was always meant to wear.' In hindsight, the

81

hope of finding the jacket was part of an elaborate architecture of self-protection: persistent hope in the face of uncertainty.

In hindsight, it felt as though I had anticipated both outcomes: on the one hand, that I actually would find the jacket, and, on the other, that I never would.

The Aura of Disappointment

But now that I have the velvet jacket, I am irrationally disappointed in it. Post-buying let-down is a common-enough feeling. However, with the jacket, this disappointment is far stronger than anything I have experienced before. Let me be clear: the jacket was all I expected it to be. But owning it did not satisfy or complete me in the way I had expected it would. I want to blame the jacket. To say: *It isn't as good as I hoped it would be*, or *My taste has changed/matured/improved*. Only none of these things are true. I just imagined I would feel different; more together; complete; of a piece. When I wasn't transformed, I felt like a failure.

In McCracken's explanation I could be Exhibit A, the classic case. The material bridge to my future self had collapsed. I now owned the object that had represented a tangible link to my ideals—even if these were, at best, vague fragments and anticipatory feelings. Possessing the jacket had not unlocked this puzzle of selfhood, and yet I was still the same person, with all the familiar doubts and ambivalences intact. Where I had previously felt the promise of the future change, I was now left holding only a piece of second-hand clothing, the smell of mothballs and disappointment heavy in the air.

The Velvet Jacket

Nothing real had, in fact, changed, except the emotional qualities evoked by the jacket were no longer present. I could now see the magical thinking that I'd drawn on to sustain hope in the face of life's difficulties. Feeling frustrated, confused and let down, I put the jacket back into the plain plastic shopping bag it came in, and hurled it into the dark recess of my wardrobe. Grant McCracken was probably right when he describes how in such moments 'when one purchases all the things that have served as bridges to displaced meaning and discovers that one's ideals remain unrealised, life is irrevocably changed'.

If disappointment kills the castles we've built in the air, what we do with it matters. Hiding the object away that has shattered our optimistic illusions is a common response to the pain of disappointed acquisition. Other strategies of self-protection include blaming the object, as I did, for failing to deliver on the easy future, or downgrading the object to a provisional status—a mere stepping stone to our 'real' wants. Some might return to the shops on a new treasure hunt, seeking distraction or a renewal of the original fantasy, through yet more anticipatory consumption. It 'seemed to me that I heard a susurration in my inner ear, telling me that something, somewhere was hanging on a rail waiting for me to meet it', writes Jenny Diski, evoking how when the 'next siren call comes, the last thing bought seems somehow not quite right'.

Diski's description is unusual for its candour, but it isn't surprising. Sociologist John Carroll points out that the occasional trip to the shopping mall isn't necessarily a problem: 'there is nothing wrong with dreaming a few escapist dreams ... The problem comes ... when more is asked of these little distractions and mild narcotics than they are up to—when they are asked to give meaning to life'. While possessing prestigious objects might help satisfy some need for attention, membership or power, its main problem for Carroll is that it does not necessarily impart meaning to one's life or help cultivate achievement of non-material goals. He contends that it is rare for material possessions to 'satisfy a deep need', except among those who went without in childhood.

Possessions, he argues, 'do not answer any essential wish, they do not water the roots of well-being'. The reason: at its core, ownership is passive—it is about having rather than doing. Simply put, no object on its own can do this job. 'At best,' argues Carroll, 'material consumption offers substitute satisfaction, a palliative to the wish to possess a thing of ultimate importance.' Shopping can be an easy, habitual and temporary fix; however, it can defer and further compound personal disappointment, leaving us with more useless stuff to hide in the wardrobe's dark corners. Fortunately, we have what the objects do not: the capacity to think, reflect and act differently.

The Biographical Object

There is no natural consequence of material disappointment, even if pushing the failed object away is a common response. I didn't have to hide my jacket in the darkness of the wardrobe. Instead I could have engaged with it, interrogated myself, to try to discover why it was an existential dead end. Instead of running from failure and becoming trapped within a cycle of wanting, buying and later discarding without end, we can explore our failed objects. What nebulous future self drew us to this ideal object in the first place?

If answering this question were easy, most of us would have already done it. I'm not convinced that there is a quick, convenient way of revealing what is opaque about our selves, like the transparency that comes with holding a piece of paper up to a window on a sunny day. Art historian Alexander Nagel, in *Women in Clothes*, suggests that while such clarity and self-awareness is the holy grail of 'style', this is a state that is felt rather than objectively known. 'I think style,' he says, 'is the state in which one feels the least separation between one's character and one's body. There is no question that style is a kind of armour.'

While style evokes a public expression of self, Jenny Diski describes the search for the 'perfect garment' as a far more private pursuit of authentic definition: 'sleuthing around the shops, I discover once again a garment that in my mind balances perfectly on the narrow boundary between inner and outer definition'. Integrity is not the word Diski uses to describe her sense of how a fashionable object can help her to feel at home in her own skin, but it seems close to what she seeks. And this, for her, is resolved in part when her private self finds expression in the material world. When her 'inner and outer definition' balance or match. 'It is,' she writes, 'an image, without any detail, of the perfect outfit, the one that slips over my frame and drapes itself over my contours in a way that finally defines me—look, this is what I am—just as my flesh defines the boundaries between myself and the world.'

What Diski describes and what I sought seems to be a variant of the 'true and false self' problem described by psychoanalyst D.W. Winnicott. While the idea of the existence of an authentic, true or core self has been criticised over the years, many of us think intuitively in these terms. The distinction captures the gap between the socially acceptable public face learned in childhood and who we are backstage, as well as the sense of knowing that we aren't likely to remain the same forever. This expresses itself in some as a concern with personal integrity, or how they can feel coherent over a lifetime. What endures, and what is essential? Winnicott sees this as a personal problem that must be lived with, but that time and maturity can 'after years and years on the horns of a dilemma' offer up this evolution, when we 'suddenly wake up and find the beast was a unicorn'.

86

Despite the promise of maturity and the limits of our self-knowledge, the object that has failed and disappointed us can offer clues about the idealised selves we seek, about where our sensibilities lie. We might, for example, ask questions: Why *this* object rather than any another? What are its qualities, and how do they speak to me? This might require allowing the object to endure in our life. Anthropologist Janet Hoskins describes two central ways in which people actually use objects in their lives. Consumers of 'public commodities are decentred and fragmented by their acquisition of things, and do not use them as part of a narrative process of self-definition'. These public (or 'protocol') objects remain impersonal. By contrast, some objects attain an intimacy in our lives whereby they become 'biographical objects' through which we 'develop ... [our] personalities and reflect on them'. At its core this once-coveted object is a question for us. It sits between who I am and know myself to be at this moment, and the person I do not know yet, but is the person who I want to become. It is an outward expression of an inward struggle.

Dim Dreams

'Vain trifles as they seem,' writes Virginia Woolf in her novel *Orlando*, 'clothes have, they say, more important offices than to merely keep us warm. They change our view of the world and the world's view of us.' While I keep the jacket out of sight for months, try as I do to ignore it, it regularly comes to my mind in the midst of doing other things. I remember that it is lurking at the back of the wardrobe. I remember my disappointment. And I remember my frustration at my inability to account for it. What changed view of myself had it held out? What sensibility did it suggest that I couldn't find elsewhere in the world?

On a sunny day, I retrieve it. I pull the jacket out of the bag. It reeks of mothballs. Impatient with myself, I Google velvet washing instructions and then, sick of my own caution, choose to ignore them. I throw the jacket in the washing machine with cold water and a goodly dose of apple-scented detergent. When I take the jacket out of the machine it looks and feels like a construction made from wet cardboard. Part of me hopes it is destroyed, while another part remains hopeful that it will come good. I hang it out to dry, and when I return it is transformed into a thing of beauty.

I try it on in front of the mirror. It smells good. It fits perfectly. Yet it does not evoke the excitement I had once anticipated it would bring. I observe my impulse to push it away. Rather than again retreating from it, I hang the jacket on my wardrobe door, where I cannot avoid it. I face it every day, for weeks and months, as I get dressed, and turn several questions over in my mind. What knot of selfhood or strand of potential did this jacket once evoke? Of all things, why *this* jacket? Where did it fit in my biography?

The jacket and its symbolism hadn't come from nowhere. As I look at it, I remember how exotic it had seemed to the quiet rural girl who first wanted it, compared to the cheap, synthetic chain-store clothing I could afford. The jacket promised not only an affordable winter alternative, but another world entirely for a girl who didn't know what she wanted, only what she didn't. It bolstered a free-floating optimism, as I faced an uncertain future. Into the jacket I poured a clichéd fantasy created from fashion magazines, divorced from any biographical reality—the fantasy was modern bohemianism.

Later on, I learn from Virginia Nicholson's insightful *Among the Bohemians* that clothing did play such a role in the lives of the British artists, writers and intellectuals of the early twentieth century. These moderns, who included artists and writers of the Bloomsbury Set, challenged the strict Victorian conventions of dress. 'From the cradle to the grave, from morning till night,' writes Nicholson, 'convention dictated what must be worn, how and with what.' The adoption of an alternative, bohemian and gypsy aesthetic released them from the 'tyranny' of clothing such as whalebone corsets, layers of woollen underwear, and excessive numbers of buttons.

Distinctive dress also had ends other than comfort and rebellion. It marked its wearer as an individual, and also as someone other artists would recognise. 'As an individual,' poet Dylan Thomas says, 'you should *look* individual, apart from the mass members of society ... I don't want to look a bit like anybody else—I couldn't if I wanted to, and I'm damned if I *do* want to'. This individuality was less idiosyncratic than Thomas's quote suggests. While it was generally opposed to the 'gutless complacency of the bourgeoisie', it also 'conferred a sense of belonging, and protective colouring'. And not just any 'camouflage' would do. The clothes the British bohemians chose to wear were often made from sensual, flowing fabrics, which responded to touch, compared to the rigid and disciplining conventional clothes. Writes Nicholson:

> Bohemia reacted to the discomfort and rigidity by choosing clothes in fluffy, comfortable fabrics. Strokeable and inviting, these shaggy tweeds, velveteens and rich corduroys implied in their fluffy depths of colour the freedom, licence and liberality of the wearer. The fact that these sensual materials quickly became shabby only added to their rather abandoned lustre.

This is not to say this pursuit of sumptuous individuality didn't become tired and worn itself. 'It was only the gullible Americans who dressed up in velveteen and *beret Basques*,' writes Nicholson, 'and got their photographs taken *en bohème*.'

My younger, teenage self who wanted the jacket had only glimpsed this history, often in glib fashion editorials. She had no real need to rebel against conservative dress— the ripped jeans and fluoro t-shirts of the 1980s had taken care of that. But she did need a prop to navigate the equally narrow ambitions of a more liberated age. This is what I suspect the jacket suggested, in my imagination at least: other ways to live a life than the main path.

Perhaps this will be dismissed as making connections where there are none to be found. The links I've made are in some ways crude and simple ones—rebellion, after all, is one of the ordinary experiences of 'interior-facing teenagery'(a wonderful phrase coined by writer Eamonn Griffin). I know that, at some basic level, my motives will remain dim and shadowed to me. And yet, I feel some relief at this understanding of the velvet jacket as a quest to reassure my younger self that my future life could be fine, even if it diverged from the dominant definitions of career success and financial achievement. I feel, as writer Rebecca Solnit puts it, a 'recognition of what has been there all along, the mystery in the middle of the room, the secret in the mirror. Sometimes one unexpected thought becomes the bridge that lets you traverse the country of the familiar in an unprecedented way'. The jacket was a bridge after all, just not the one I thought it would be. And after this insight, the jacket became just a jacket.

Becoming

The easy daydream of one day finding an object you want is a consoling, seemingly harmless delusion. It tacks together two events: the lucky find, on the one hand, and the day when everything will slot into place, on the other. The latter is the day when you no longer will be a puzzle to yourself. An object might provide the clues: not so much to who you are, but who you would like to be. Artist and writer Edmund de Waal, drawing on poet Paul

The Velvet Jacket

Celan's lecture on poetry, uses the following evocative phrase: 'you send yourself ahead, in search of yourself'. This is what the grasping for identity through objects feels like. The mistake, though, is assuming that this one action of acquisition will allow us to find and become this future self.

But the inanimate object cannot, of course, do this work for us. The intriguing, the beautiful, and the coveted object can suggest this future and give it an aspect of tangible reality, but it is only us who can do the difficult practical, emotional and psychological work to bridge the gap between optimistic hopes and reality, to close the gap between Winnicott's 'false' and 'true' selves. This is predictably difficult. Disappointments in the object are reminders of how far we have to go, how much we have to still discover about our 'dim dreams'.

Simone de Beauvoir's Bicycle

It's a new joy in life that I've discovered and, instead of wishing for a car, my desires will henceforth be limited to a bicycle of my own.
Simone de Beauvoir's letter to Jean-Paul Sartre,
Monday 29 July 1940

Personal property is important precisely because its holder could not be the particular person she is without it.
Margaret Radin, *Reinterpreting Property*

The Novice

It is one of the first days of the northern hemisphere's summer, on a warm July afternoon. The year is 1940 and a 32-year-old teacher called Simone de Beauvoir is learning to ride on a borrowed bicycle. She is on Paris's quiet backstreets, and takes to it quickly, much to her surprise. That evening she confides in her diary, with pride, how 'on the first try I stayed on the seat and even learned to get on alone and make turns'. At this point, though, her literary success and celebrity are still several years away. 'I had not yet published,' she later reflects, 'and no one thought of me as anything more than "Sartre's girlfriend".' On that July day, she was just another novice cyclist learning to get the hang of balancing on two wheels, while trying to coordinate pushing the pedals at the same time.

De Beauvoir was late to cycling, even though many women, especially American feminists, had been cycling for decades. ('Let me tell you what I think of bicycling,' early American feminist Susan B. Anthony apparently said in an 1896 interview, 'I think it has done more to emancipate women than anything else in the world ... It gives woman a *feeling* of freedom and self-reliance. It makes her feel as if she were independent.') It was not fear or convention that blocked de Beauvoir's way, but money. Her father had wanted to buy bicycles for his two daughters, Simone and her younger sister, Hélène, when they were children, but their mother was concerned about the family's precarious finances. She missed the early joys of riding because her family just could not afford the luxury of bicycles.

This delay did not, however, diminish her immediate elation at learning to ride as an adult. In her wartime diary she records in detail not only the ease with which she learned, but also the delight she took in her own achievement. She was quickly hooked. 'I went to get her bicycle, and for an hour I rode it around, to the Parc Montsouris and back, then to the Closerie des Lilas and back,' she writes. 'I really handled it with ease, except one time I crashed into a dog and another time I collided with two women, and I was very happy.' Soon she was chasing this experience, day after day.

De Beauvoir's account evokes what I've almost for-gotten about learning to ride a bike. I remember I scraped my toes using them to brake. But the strongest feeling is of finally having enough control over the handlebars and peddles to ride independently. The power I felt when I no longer needed anyone's help to stay upright, or push me along. How I could then ride, within reason, where I wanted, when I wanted, as fast as my legs could make the chain turn on my yellow and black BMX. It was exhilarating.

But de Beauvoir wasn't doing laps around her back garden. She was riding without any explicit purpose in a city occupied by German troops, their trucks rolling into its streets. When she briefly left Paris ahead of the occupying troops, her landlady threw most of her possessions away—she did not expect de Beauvoir to return. In her diary, de Beauvoir seems indifferent to their loss. But the bicycle was a different matter. It became what her biographer, Deirdre Bair, describes as 'her most treasured possession throughout the war'.

The People's Nag

As a rider, I want to know about the details of Simone de Beauvoir's bicycle: whether its paintwork was bold or plain, if its chrome was gleaming or rusty, if its leather seat had an elegant design. Or better still, I'd like to tell you that the original was found at the back of a dusty farmyard shed in the French countryside, or chanced upon at a flea market (perhaps along with one of de Beauvoir's stylish turbans). But, to my knowledge, no such bicycle has been found. The only thing that we do know is that it was borrowed from Nathalie Sorokine and, as in *The Blood of Others*, it was most likely stolen. (In a thriving wartime black market for bicycles, Sorokine was an enthusiastic and successful thief.)

The Promise of Things

The absence of de Beauvoir's bicycle bothers me. Despite her diligent diary notes, why didn't de Beauvoir describe the bicycle itself? Possibly because it was so commonplace that she felt it needed no description. Bicycles at the time were more common than today, with millions produced every year in Europe's bicycle workshops, including the French cycling capital, Saint-Étienne. There, according to bicycle historian David V. Herlihy, 'more than a hundred bicycle-related firms … together produced 80 percent of the country's output.' It's likely that de Beauvoir's borrowed bicycle was just another of the millions of bicycles on the streets, especially as fuel was in short supply.

But the fantasy persists that this most treasured possession was one unique bicycle, rather than a serial object indistinguishable from any other. De Beauvoir's own fictionalised account of a coveted bicycle, in the wartime novel *The Blood of Others*, on first reading fuels this belief. 'The bicycle was still there, brand new,' the young bicycle thief Hélène observes, as she covets her neighbour's new steel and chrome bicycle with its 'pale-blue frame and its plated handlebars', gleaming mudguards and fat tyres.

Yet, read on carefully and it is clear that the beauty of the bicycle is tied to what it promises Hélène: freedom of movement. She anticipates what possessing it would feel like: 'It must be heavenly to sit on that beautiful yellow saddle and grip the handlebars in one's hands!' If she had it, she could 'go everywhere I want. I'll come home late at night. Only a pool of light will go ahead of me in the silent streets.' At the heart of the bicycle's significance isn't one particular bicycle, but what possessing any bicycle would allow her—de Beauvoir as much as Hélène—to do.

Objects of Freedom

A stereo in a teenager's bedroom.

> The woodworking tools in the garage.
>
> A camera used on the weekends.
>
> A musical instrument in the basement.
>
> A bicycle in wartime.

Some of the objects that we most value do not have a high monetary or even sentimental value. Rather, we value them for what we can do with them, and the experiences that they, and only they, can offer us. They each, like the bicycle and the car de Beauvoir had previously wanted, offer an experience of control over our lives, even if this is limited in scope. For rebelling teenagers, employees in difficult jobs, and the middle-aged feeling the weight of family and professional responsibilities, such objects can provide an arena of free choice or escape. But how do such objects make us feel free?

A possession is a 'right to action', as sociologist Lewis Hyde summarises it in *The Gift*. When we possess an object it is ours to do what we choose with, from using to selling, from giving away to destroying (as artist Michael Landy chose to do in *Break Down*). As Hyde puts it, 'a thing (or a person) becomes a "property" whenever someone has "in it" the right of any such action. There is no property without an actor.' Hyde's 'old definition' has echoes in contemporary property law, where a possession retains this quality of not merely being an object that is owned, but something that is actively possessed and intentionally controlled.

Legal scholar Margaret Radin draws on philosopher Georg Hegel's *Philosophy of Right* to explain the centrality of human will—the intersection of property and personhood—in this understanding. Hegel argues that a person's will can be placed in 'any and every thing', and because a thing has 'no end in itself, its destiny and soul take on my will'. Yet this interaction is not all one way, for two reasons. First, many objects are designed to have an end, especially utilitarian objects. We cannot impose our 'right to action' over them in any way we choose. We do not have omnipotent control over the object possessed, however much we might like this to be the case. Secondly, as Radin points out, personal property influences our lives and experiences in such a way that we cannot be the person we are without it. Some objects become imprinted on, and intertwined with, our experiences and our identities, to the extent that while they remain ultimately separable, estrangement can cause us pain or damage.

This does not happen automatically. While tools can set the parameters of action in this way, this is not a one-way relationship. 'The "thing",' argues sociologist Tim Dant, 'is an active part of the experience … [and] cannot be treated as mere thing; as inanimate, inert, incapable'. I cannot, for instance, use a hammer in any way I like. There is a correct way to hold the handle, a way to line up the nail and swing the hammer effectively. And, as many 5-year-olds quickly discover, there is a correct way to ride a bike that you cannot think your way into. It requires learning how to balance, how to keep momentum going forward, and necessitates that the rider learns the embodied knack of working in concert with the bicycle. In this way, the bicycle mediates, restricts and shapes how we ride.

'The thing,' as Dant continues, 'offers a set of possible lines of action and limitations on action.' In this interaction with the object, the user and object temporarily join, and the tool becomes an extension of its user. This can be seen in the dance between many objects and users: the musician's will and his guitar, the carpenter's intention and her saw, the skater's ambition and his board. It is often most obvious with the amateur, such as the novice windsurfer who keeps climbing back on her board, when the relationship between person and tool is not taken for granted and rendered second nature. And it is this interaction, argues psychologist Mihaly Csikszentmihalyi, 'that produces a rare unity with these usually foreign entities'. Dant calls this the 'seduction of the object … [object], which holds out to us the promise of merger', through which we might become a 'different being'. Writer Robert Penn invokes a similar idea when he calls the bicycle the 'unifying thing' that brings the rider and her experiences together. It is this compelling, unexpected 'promise of merger' that I suspect drove de Beauvoir's riding. This promise, when it is realised, is found in the playing.

This merger can amplify our abilities, strengths and capacities, or aid us to transcend our limitations, so that we enjoy not only the expression of our will in the world, but feel our powers heightened and intensified. And this relationship confers other benefits. A woman in a country possessed and controlled by an enemy army might, in some limited way, experience her own autonomy and liberty of movement aboard a bicycle. This is certainly what de Beauvoir describes.

Even in today's technologically developed world, the human-powered bicycle still offers independent mobility, and often leaves the rider with a feeling of freedom and adventure. Like other tools, the bicycle heightens, extends and expands the capacity of the human body. On board, you can travel faster, over longer distances. The specifics of this practical contribution are important. Penn, in his book on the happiness of cycling, *It's All About the Bike*, says of the bicycle, 'it can be ridden, on a reasonable surface, at four or five times the pace of walking, with the same amount of effort—making it the most efficient, self-powered means of transportation ever invented'.

When everything about a mechanical object or tool works as it should, we might call this object beautiful. This link between function and beauty is often made by abbreviating 'It works beautifully' to 'It is beautiful'. And this leap is not at all unusual. Architecture and interior design writer Stanley Abercrombie argues in *Work, Life, Tools* that 'we expect our tools to be pretty ... because of an inherent fitness to purpose that, we have learned to expect, results in beauty.'

For Its Own Sake

There is another pleasure of objects over and above the expression of will, the extension of our powers, and the beauty of use: play. De Beauvoir was a fast learner. 'I was very proud and it was fun,' she writes of her first ride. Chasing this novel experience got her out of bed early in the mornings, even though she was a late sleeper and her mood was low. 'I woke up at eight o'clock, still a little sleepy,' she writes on Wednesday 10 July, 'but I got up because I wanted to go on a long bicycle ride.' She could easily have retreated under the blankets and hidden from the world. And, she didn't necessarily have anywhere to go. I suspect she was doing what so many weekend cyclists, hobbyists, and amateurs do: finding a space to play, away from the bad news that threatened to overwhelm her. 'Sometimes,' writes Robert Penn, 'I ride my bicycle just to ride my bicycle.'

Play is often thought of as belonging only to the world of children—it's often said that a child's 'job' is to play. Children learn many things through their primary, often tactile, engagement with the material world: banging rattles, stacking blocks, and later imitating the adult world with toy tea sets and plastic vegetables. Once at school, they learn about cooperation and competition in the safety of the secondary world of games, with formal rules, such as netball and cricket.

Play, however, often disappears for adults. Family, career and financial obligations leave little to no time for the unproductive play of childhood. I regularly hear myself saying to my own children that I haven't time to play. Adult play has become the domain of professional sports players who can combine earnings with skill. But this is a new phenomenon. Leisure, as writer and architect Witold Rybczynski characterises it in *The Atlantic*, was once 'the opportunity for personal, even idiosyncratic, pursuits, not for ordered recreation ... for private reveries rather than for public spectacles'.

Like daydreaming and reverie, free play is open-ended and useless. To play is to freely engage in an activity that is 'spectacular or ostentatious', as French sociologist Roger Caillois puts it. In play, nothing is produced, but energy is expended. Play, as Caillois puts it, 'creates no wealth or goods', but its rather 'an occasion of pure waste: waste of time, energy, ingenuity, skill'. As such, play stands in stark contrast to working life, where our labours and time are

101

expected to be timed, measurably productive, efficient and effective. Play, however, is not only separated from work but also, suggests Caillois, 'carefully isolated from the rest of life, and generally engaged in with precise limits of time and place'.

Caillois identifies four different domains of play, each of which allows us to escape the 'real world' and experience particular pleasures. In *Agôn* types of play we get to experience competition, such as in team sports; in *Alea* play, such as card games, all is chance. *Mimicry*, such as childhood dress-ups, is playing different roles. Finally, there is *Ilinx* play, which is active play that can 'momentarily destroy the stability of perception and inflict a kind of voluptuous panic upon an otherwise lucid mind'. For the child, Ilinx is found in the dizzy-whizzy or cartwheel. Sociologists Norbert Elias and Eric Dunning describe such activity as the human need for elementary excitement. The adult equivalent is teetering on the edge of control, often aboard some kind of wheels: rollerskates, scooters, skateboards and bikes. Writer Jack London vividly evokes this type of experience: 'Ever bike? Now that's what makes life worth living! ... Oh, to just grip your handlebars and lay down to it'.

Feeling Free

On her first morning in occupied Paris, de Beauvoir awoke 'feeling more miserable than I had in my entire life'. Just getting around the city was now difficult. In her diary she recounts walking twenty-five miles to visit her lover Bost's family and 'bravely walking back despite my ill-fitting shoes'. The trip had failed to yield any word about the captured soldiers, Bost and Sartre. And she had failed in her plan to hitch a return lift. Even sleep offered no refuge—she dreamed Sartre wanted to strangle her. It is no exaggeration to say that she felt trapped, alienated and despairing. Her mood, she writes, was dark. Yet, the ordinary elements of life continued despite the long shadow cast by the occupation. After work, lunch with family, and writing, de Beauvoir made room for cycling. 'I went back to the Deux Magots to read and write to Kos; then from five to six I rode my bicycle,' wrote de Beauvoir on Thursday 4 July 1940, 'with fun, fatigue and success'.

Why, though, play as an adult, by riding a bicycle during an enemy occupation? When we engage in rich, intense and voluntary activities, we lose track of the everyday world and its demands. As psychologist Mihaly Csikszentmihalyi puts it (when summarising the empirical evidence for, and philosophical significance of, intrinsic motivation) 'freedom is the essential criterion of an enjoyable act. It is for this reason that thinkers like Heraclitus, Plato, Nietzsche, and Sartre have held play in such high esteem: Play is an activity that one is free to enter and free to leave'. In her diary, de Beauvoir describes the hidden psychological shift within her after the occupation. Yet, aboard the bicycle she could feel 'happiness' and 'joy'. While riding, she felt unexpectedly transformed, taken out of herself and the situation. She was not only temporarily removed from the pressures of life under occupation, but also left feeling stronger, physically and psychologically, and better equipped to deal with her circumstances. In fact, the bicycle experience was significant enough to displace her longing for a car, and for her to put this in a letter to her partner, Jean-Paul Sartre, who at the time was being held by the Germans as a prisoner of war.

Even in less dire times, objects can evoke the feeling of being free, even when we are objectively constrained, they are reminders of freedom. They are often associated not with paid labour, but with enjoyable leisure or creative work. Even when not in use, they seem to hold the door mentally ajar for their owners. Not to run away and escape their lives, but rather to leave open the possibility that they are not wholly determined and sentenced to simply live out their fate. In this sense, their presence can create a little existential wiggle room. A contemporary example of this comes from one-time lawyer Robert Penn, who describes how his old mountain bike held his adventurous past as a tangible alternative to London lawyerhood. 'I rode it from Kashgur in China to Peshawar in Pakistan, over the Karakoram mountains and the Hindu Kush,' he recounts. 'When I was back in London, working as a lawyer, the Saracen [bike] more than carried me around: it represented life beyond the pinstripe suit. Then it got stolen.' (Bicycle theft remains as endemic as it was in de Beauvoir's day.)

The object also provides a socially acceptable and recognisable link to play—a reminder for the self and others. The social acceptability of thousands of weekend cyclists depends upon this thing called a bike and the practices of cycling associated with it. The same goes for other objects we draw on to cultivate and express our selves: cameras, tools, musical instruments and the things we create with them. Even though our instrumental objects, such as tools, are 'limited in space and time', writes Stanley Abercrombie, 'they are still more real and more permanent than some of the things they help to make'. The feeling of creative labour or free play produced in their use is ephemeral. The object, in its concreteness, gives a tangible link to what we cannot hold firm in our grasp. The object becomes a symbol—a way to keep this feeling fresh in our mind.

Importantly, this felt or subjective freedom is not a solution to objective constraints. It is not substantive freedom of the enfranchised political type or the kind associated with unlimited economic choices. Nor is it the absolute freedom that might come to a sulky child's mind who dreams of being liberated from all rules, laws or obligations. It is simply the situated feeling of being unshackled, more autonomous, more self-reliant, and engaged in something worth doing for its own sake.

Advertisers also know we love this sense of freedom. They regularly bait their hooks with its promise to sell everything from cars to bikes, from cameras to beach umbrellas. When we buy these objects, we are often buying the promise they represent of time and energy, rather like the stylised, casual picnic in magazines represents carefree enjoyment.

The Force of Circumstance

Simone de Beauvoir did not know what the future held for her. In July 1940, German troops were on the streets of her city. She could find no news of her partner, Jean-Paul Sartre, or her lover, Jacques-Laurent Bost. Food and fuel shortages were beginning to hit Paris. This had caught de Beauvoir unawares. She had not expected the war to last longer than a year. Her first response to this new situation had been to flee Paris ahead of the invading army, and take refuge in the countryside. Once there, she escaped into the safety of reading detective novels, but this did not last. She described herself as reduced to living like a 'crushed bug' rather than a full person. While she remained ostensibly free, the future seemed closed to her. There was no longer, in her words, a 'shining moment on the horizon to which one could offer up the present—there was now more waiting, no more future'.

Unexpectedly, the stolen bicycle offered her a space in which she felt free to act. With this object she could extend her body and claim a greater liberty of movement. Of course, the bicycle didn't change or completely block out the world around her. But it did offer her a new experience of herself within these new constraints. 'I rolled along and was enchanted to be able to go on a real outing. I arrived in Auteuil tired and content,' she wrote. 'I loved hearing music and the entire afternoon made up a happy whole. [Reading] Hegel, bicycle, music—but interrupted by frightening German chatter.'

The rights of action claimed through possessions can be quite humble. We are not all powerful, and our lives are usually not lived entirely as we choose. Yet the objects we own can aid us to express our will in this world, to put our intentions into action, and to claim the modest freedoms that have been there all along. This is their promise, but it requires us to animate them. Like the 'faithful and obedient' bicycle parked on the curb side in de Beauvoir's *The Blood of Others*, our objects will be there, waiting for us to realise this promise.

The Singer Sewing Machine

*The craftsman is proud of what he has made, and cherishes it, while
the consumer discards things that are perfectly serviceable in his
restless pursuit of the new. The craftsman is then more possessive,
more tied to what is present, the dead incarnation of past labour;
the consumer is more free, more imaginative, and so more valorous
according to those who would sell us things.*
Philosopher Matthew Crawford, *Shop Class as Soulcraft*

The Making

The Singer I sit at is heavy with my nostalgia for the past.
It is not an electric white plastic one. It is a beautiful,
old, foot-powered machine, approaching its centenary. A
piece of the past anchoring the fast-shifting present. The
Singer is a heavy, black iron machine, decorated with
ornate gold swirls, which sits atop a robust, wrought-iron
base. The base bears the manufacturer's distinctive sig-
nature. It contrasts against the warmth of the oak veneer
of the wooden top, which folds out, and the six small
drawers, which ought to contain pins, cottons and other
sewing paraphernalia, but more often hide my son's toy
steam trains. The machine quietly trundles along as I rock
my foot on the treadle. But this is not strictly about the

sewing machine. It is a path to another object that does not yet exist: the one I am making. Or, more accurately, attempting to make. The outcome is not assured.

I place the fabric into position, and lower the small steel foot. I stitch forward a little, and then backwards, as I was taught to do when I was a child. I stitch forward again until I come to the corner of what I hope will soon become a long, pointy rabbit ear. I stop, lift the foot, turn the fabric at a sharp angle, secure the foot again, and stitch until the raw edge. I feel optimistic. One part down, only the rest to go. I continue sewing, at first patiently around sharp corners and curves, then with mounting frustration as I coax the thick seams together, making it take the shape I have in my mind: a stuffed toy rabbit, a simple gift for my youngest's first birthday. And, hastily, another one in response to my 4-year-old son's plaintive question: '*When will you make mine?*'

This is hands-on work, but it is guided by experience and judgements. The actions I repeat again and again are taken in concert with unseen mental work about how much I can push thread, needle and material. Not that you'd know it. As I sit at the old treadle by the sunny bedroom window on the first day of my annual leave, I look like, depending on your perspective, either the ideal of creative maternal tranquillity, or the embodiment of trivial 'women's work'. Possibly both. The outcome, though, will be undeniably tangible, even if the result is a ball of rags that stands testament to the failure of my attempt.

Yet, as the parent of two children under five, suffering from their interrupted sleep patterns and my own flagging energy, it makes little rational sense for me to be making these rabbits myself. I could easily save myself the time, effort and uncertainty. Why make a gift when I could pop around to the toy shop on the corner and buy a similar one? It isn't like my young daughter would know the difference. And the quality would most likely be better than my amateur work. Or I could go to a big chain store and buy a popular Disney or Lego toy for my son. Perhaps I could even buy them two toys each for the same price as the time I'd spent making one.

The economics and ease are passing deliberations, quickly dismissed. Instead, I stay up by lamplight, hand-embroidering the rabbits' rust-pink noses and black felt eyes. What is it about the handmade object, whether purchased or DIY, that makes it special? What hunger, need or promise does it fill that the mass produced cannot? And why, in this time of mass abundance, is the handmade popular again?

109

A Popular Renaissance

'Handmade' was once a euphemism for something that was inferior, cringeworthy or desperate. While professional dressmakers, lacemakers and smockers often made bespoke pieces with their highly skilled hands, 'handmade' more often brought to mind the unpolished amateur, frugally making ends meet. It was more likely to evoke a well-meaning nanna armed with a Bedazzler or crochet hook, or a teenager with a not-quite-right pinch pot, rather than an artisan in her white studio with a 3D printer and website. In contrast to the shop-bought equivalent, the handmade lacked gloss, sophistication and, importantly, ease: the ease to buy, and with it the ease to discard.

The Promise of Things

Around the turn of the new millennium, the image of the handmade began to noticeably change and to enjoy a popular renaissance. This is true of traditional making practices in general, like baking, home-brewing and vegetable gardening. While this rebirth of the handmade is not easily reducible to a certain look or style, a deep vein of cheerful nostalgia for 'simpler times' ran through it: faded vintage fabrics, quaint stuffed toys without batteries, humble pillowslip dresses without brands, colourful bunting. Gone were the frugal browns and tweeds of the 1970s handmade tradition. Now the library and bookshop shelves were stocked with contemporary crafting books and magazines that nodded to the 1950s' optimism.

Yet, the most quantifiable indicator of the appetite for the handmade wasn't local or old-fashioned at all. It was online. In 2005, Etsy arrived. The success of Etsy, a Brooklyn-based online sales platform for vintage and handmade objects, reveals what was largely hidden: the extent of handmade appeal. By 2010, Etsy had 1.4 million sellers who sold objects to 19.8 million buyers worldwide. Just four years later, it had US$2 billion sales, with almost one in three sellers outside the United States.

Etsy's success is mirrored in other sites. In Britain, Folksy, the online market for British-made handcrafts and design, has sold over a million pounds' worth of goods since commencing business in 2008. At the time of writing, it has 166 536 objects for sale from 5763 designers and makers. A report for the London-based Crafts Council in 2010 found stronger evidence of this trend, with an estimated 5.6 million craft objects being bought every year by people who live in England, with two in five adults (16.9 million people) having previously bought a craft object. In Australia, there are no fewer than three online marketplaces for handmade goods: madeit, Hand-Made, and Handmade HQ, in addition to markets, fairs and retailers of handmade objects. One of these Australian websites alone, madeit, had 6700 active sellers in 2015.

But buying isn't the only expression of interest in the handmade. Its rediscovery coincides with a renewal of interest in making itself. No longer driven by the necessity of making do and mending, amateur handmaking and craft participation have become the surprise popular leisure-time activities of the early twenty-first century. One in every ten Australians over the age of fifteen years takes part in a classic craft activity, including textile crafts like sewing, knitting and felting, and manual crafts, like jewellery making, decoupage and wood crafts, with 1.3 million women and 532 000 men freely involved in making in their leisure time, such as on weekends or evenings, according to the Australian Bureau of Statistics. And this is on the increase. According to writer Ben Eltham's analysis, general craft participation in the six years from 2001 to 2007 almost tripled from 396 400 to 960 800 people, with jewellery making having the most rapid increase, from 25 000 to 193 000. Not surprisingly, the industries that support these leisure-time pursuits are worth billions of dollars. In the United States, for instance, the needle crafts industry alone is worth US$2.9 billion dollars, according to the US Craft and Hobby Association.

What is driving this new interest in handmade things? Is it the objects themselves, or something beyond them?

Hands On

'Smooth, shiny and uniform is now equated with cheap, especially when compared with the individuality of hand-crafted products,' argues futurist and trend forecaster Faith Popcorn. 'We are hungry,' she continues, 'for things that have touched human hands.' The most frequent explanation is that the handmade object has something intrinsic that the mass-produced lacks. But what exactly?

In Popcorn's formulation, the reason is simple: the 'smooth, shiny and uniform' is deficient. This is not a new criticism of the mass-manufactured object. Nineteenth-century writers, such as John Ruskin and William Morris, worried that a world of uniform mass-produced objects would diminish our sensory engagement, leaving us craving material variation and discovery. 'For the first time,' writes sociologist Richard Sennett, summarising the Victorians' fears about the impact of mechanisation of production, 'the sheer quantity of uniform objects aroused concerns that numbers would dull the senses, the uniform perfection of machine goods issuing no sympathetic invitation, no personal response.'

While this concern went away for a while, it has re-emerged at a time of other anxieties in the era of globalisation. More recently, senior curator of decorative arts and design at the National Gallery of Australia Robert Bell offered a similar, more contemporary take on the aesthetic case, arguing that it is the nuances of handmaking that find their way into the finished object that make these objects more compelling than their mass rivals. 'The handmade,' he writes, 'comes with a nervous uncertainty that allows it to transcend the merely fashionable, to posit a set of values that must be encountered, if not embraced, before hidden subtleties can be contemplated.' 'Nervous uncertainty', unpredictability, and sensory distinctiveness are sources of enrichment awaiting those individuals who are discerning, sensitive and patient enough to find them.

And yet, today's mass objects are by no means all smooth and shiny. They do not announce themselves as mass objects. Some successfully ape the sensory variation of the potter's wheel, or village embroidery. It is difficult to automatically know the mass from the authentically handmade. And this boundary is often a blurry one. Why, then, all this bother with the handmade?

Popcorn's 'human hands' formulation, though, isn't strictly about aesthetic appetite for the authentic, or superior sensory rewards. It is about the pursuit of exclusivity. For Popcorn, the chief deficiency of the mass object in a social one. Mass manufacture has achieved the feat of being able to meet most human needs. Each year, for instance, twelve and a half billion pairs of shoes are made in China. Enough, as journalist Matt Schiavenza writing for *The Atlantic* points out, 'for every man, woman, and child in the world to have two'. But this achievement undermines another 'need'—the individual's need for distinction.

At its crudest, the quest for distinction through connoisseurship of the handmade is the materialistic individual's striving for recognition, status or distinction through things. At its more nuanced, it is the pursuit of individuality and personal expressiveness, a desire that may be intensified in the climate of mass sameness and standardisation spread by advanced capitalism—a logic that, as geographer David Harvey puts it, 'ends up putting Benetton or Laura Ashley products in almost every serially produced shopping mall in the advanced capitalist world'.

Yet, these two explanations are not compelling or comprehensive enough to account for the handmade object's new popularity. Surely there is more to our hunger for 'human hands'.

Whose Hands?

The rabbits are finished. In the morning, I examine the handiwork from the late night before. The rabbits' arms and legs flop in a satisfying way, ready to fold into a clumsy embrace, or collapse sprawled out on the floor. Their heads are firm and well shaped from being stuffed full with scraps—strong enough to withstand the bites to come from a teething toddler. Each robust face has a reassuring structure, enigmatic black felt eyes and embroidered rust-pink nose. A simple line of the rust-pink running stitch adds definition to their unstuffed ears, making them stick up. They bear the marks of the decisions that I made along the way, the marks of me as their maker, for good and for ill.

Richard Sennett describes the marks left by makers on objects—often left intentionally—as makers' marks. They are simple statements 'imposed on inert materials'. They say 'I made this', 'I am here, in this work', 'I exist'. They are 'primal' messages of presence. And, whatever the rabbits' failings, they bear mine. I am here *in* them. They are evidence of my own free labour. They are mine to give.

Human hands just like mine are present throughout mass production. It is a mistake to assume it is mostly mechanised—the fantasy of robot arms doing all the productive work. Hands are especially fundamental to the making of textiles, even if parts of the process are automated or produced by multiple workers. The workers' hands and their labour, however, are anonymous and alienated from what they create. As philosopher Karl Marx put it, 'the worker is related to the product of his labour as to an alien object'. And we are, in turn, alienated from the producers of these objects through the production process. By the time these objects reach the shops as commodities, any sign of the distinct maker's presence has been dimmed or erased.

This is the logical consequence of standardised mass production. Our alienation from these hands is further intensified by the fact that production no longer happens locally on the outskirts of the suburbs or in rag-trade laneways. Global chains of production seeking low labour costs means making happens thousands of kilometres removed from the people who buy the end products. For example, over a decade ago, writer Isabel Hilton, in an essay for *Granta* magazine, observed how Guangdong Province in China produced a vast chunk of the world's objects, including 'two-thirds of the world's photocopiers, microwave ovens, DVD players and shoes, more than half of the world's digital cameras and two-fifths of its personal computers'. As Hilton puts it: 'Guangdong's business is to make things'.

This has consequences for how we relate to these objects. The anonymity of labour, in concert with its low cost, helps to disburden us, to use philosopher Matthew Crawford's phrase, of a potentially deeper layer of involvement with the object. The object becomes less than the

115

sum of its parts. But doubts linger. The goods are cheap but are they a good deal? When news breaks, as it regularly does, of exploitative working conditions, or deaths in factories, or asbestos in children's crayons, we as distant consumers are often horrified. It reveals how impotent we have become to change these things that happen at arm's length from our everyday lives. It reinforces what we already suspect: how we have become buyers, rather than makers, or as Hilton points out, dependent end-stage users in a system that only works for us for now. For now. Deep down, we suspect that this is only provisional.

The West's need for 'human hands' exists in a more complicated relationship to a broader system of labour and production. By contrast, the handmade object resists this system and the anonymity and distance upon which it pivots. The handmade, instead, invites us to deepen our involvement with the object, and to imagine the specifics of its creation: Whose hands? Where? Under what conditions? With what identities and rhythms?

Imagined Hands

'This might sound weird,' environmental writer Tanya Ha wrote recently, 'but I sometimes like to close my eyes, touch a favourite garment and try to imagine all the hands that touched and made the garment, from the farmer who grew the fibre, through the many stages of manufacture, finally to me.' It is a challenging thought experiment to imagine the chain of human hands that have produced most of the objects that populate our homes and offices. Ha is doing the imaginative work that underpins what some have called the 'responsibility revolution'. This type of thinking connects a broad range of concerns about the social, political, environmental and ethical consequences bound up in our consumption. Within this diverse 'revolution', the handmade object offers a quiet form of resistance. 'In a time of over-ease and overuse and overspending,' says sociologist and activist Betty Greer, 'I can take back control of where my money goes, over what my outfit is, and over how my life is lived'.

Responses to global chains of production and the uncertainty they produce often, as geographer David Harvey identifies, involve two approaches. The first is to look to the past for existential security, and the second is to turn to the local for a sensibility that stands outside the global market. In the local we hope to find qualities that are distinctive, unique and, most crucially, outside the homogenous world of the serial shopping mall where, as the London-based Crafts Council puts it, 'anything is available, anywhere, through globalised distribution systems'. Often, the handmade object offers both: a nostalgic nod to the faded certainties of the 1950s and 1960s, through the work of a local maker.

The Handmade Effect

While hand- and mass-made objects both typically involve human hands in concert with technology, such as sewing machines, handmaking evokes an ideal working environment. The chief hallmark of the handmade is not the presence of hands or the absence of machines, as sociologist Colin Campbell observes, but rather who controls the machine and under what conditions. The handmaker has control over what, when and how she sews, while the

117

factory machinist sews at the behest of the factory system. Her sewing tasks are to suit the factory, and are likely to be compartmentalised into repetitive piecework such as the sewing of zips or hems. The handmaker has what the factory worker does not: autonomy, control and the satisfaction of completing a whole project from beginning to end.

But even here the line is blurred by the market. In 2013, the online handmade retailer Etsy reconceptualised what it would call handmade. This controversial expansion of its definition now includes makers who hire staff to manufacture and ship goods. 'We choose to define handmade,' says Etsy's Nicole Vanderbilt in *Mollie Makes* magazine, 'as a set of values, and not as a particular method or process.' Whose hands made the handmade object can no longer be taken for granted.

Despite this recent grabbling over the definition, the term handmade still evokes an ideal of liberated creative labour, with hands working to their own rhythms, with the finished objects reflecting the distinctive identity of their makers. Handmade is deeply evocative of skill, craft, creativity and freedom. 'Handmade', as Geoff Slattery, the publisher of the directory *Handmade in Melbourne*, writes, 'is a wonderfully descriptive term. It evokes a sense of total creativity, the capacity to turn common ingredients or materials into something of purpose, and often of great beauty. It's a rare skill to be able to achieve both.'

And this has a very real impact on potential buyers and consumers of handmade objects. The term 'handmade effect' was recently coined by marketing academics Christopher Fuchs, Martin Schreier and Stijn M. J. van Osselaer to explain their findings in three countries:

Austria, the Netherlands and the United States. They found that not only were handmade objects seen as more attractive by consumers than objects of an unknown origin, consumers were prepared to pay significantly more for them, especially when buying a gift for someone they love. This overturns the classic assumptions of consumers as either rational economic decision-makers seeking the 'best deal', or dupes conned by advertising.

What accounts for this 'handmade effect'?

Fuchs and his colleagues' belief is that the people project positive meanings onto the handmade object. Instead of neutrally evaluating the handmade object on its own terms, as rational economic decision-makers are expected to do, they imbue the object with beliefs about the person who made it. They value the object by what they cannot see, but assume to be true, about the object being freely made as a labour of love, skill and creativity. As with physical contagion, some essence of the maker is believed to adhere to the object from being made by their particular human hands. The object catches something of the person who made it. 'Touched by human hands' evokes a fantasy in the buyer's mind of a real maker with a singular consciousness.

This positive contagion is reinforced by direct contact with makers. Etsy CEO Chad Dickerson even identifies this direct relationship between the buyer and seller of the handmade product as crucial to his company's success. 'At the end of every transaction,' Dickerson said in a 2013 interview, 'you get something real from a real person. There is an existential satisfaction to that.' In this way, the handmade object is a consolation for a largely alienating, consumerist world.

Handmade Comforts

Why seek consolation in the handmade? The popularity of handmade objects, alongside amateur handmaking, is explained by some as an expression of what is missing in many of our working lives. No longer immune to global patterns and trends, no longer able to take for granted a job for life, our lives feel unpredictable, risky and slightly beyond our control. In response to this, buying or creating handmade objects is an escape. The objects answer to a deep human need for what philosopher Matthew Crawford calls an 'intelligible world'. The 'poignant longing for responsibility that many people experience in their home lives may be (in part),' argues Crawford, 'a response to changes in the world of work, where the experience of human agency has become elusive'. American crafter and documentary filmmaker Faythe Levine in *Handmade Nation: The Rise of DIY, Art, Craft, and Design* describes developing traditional skills and being part of a craft community as crucial to 'having control over my life. I am making my destiny with what I create'. Making allows her to feel she is an active agent.

Colin Campbell of the University of York suggests that it is educated, middle-class and professional groups in particular who are most keenly feeling the loss of their status, vocations and stability. And it is this group's response to losses in their professional lives during late capitalism that may account for the rise in popularity of the handmade, do it yourself, or post-consumption modifying of bought objects. Workers seek in the 'private sphere just those satisfactions that they find no longer available to them in the public one ... divert[ing] the creative human energies that were formerly expressed in the world of work into the world of leisure'. Craft participation and consumption, alongside the valuing of traditional skills, speaks to longings for stability and enduring value. These longings might be particularly acute among the professionals in the midst of de-skilling, if only as distractions, consolations, or leisure-time retreats from the dissatisfactions of work-aday life.

Betty Greer, for instance, links her alienation as a dull day-job worker answering phones in an office cubicle, to her initial impetus to knit: 'the thought of learning something new that I could continue to improve on for decades and learning something that would bring me solace ... and keep my hands busy ... was exciting'. It might also come to represent the only realisation of her labour in a tangible object. Realisation, as philosopher Karl Marx puts it, is 'accomplishment, performance, making something real'. The created object might well come to stand as material evidence of skilled, creative and free labour—evidence of our existence lacking or without an outlet in modern work. 'As an everyday hobby,' write researchers Elizabeth Goodman and Daniela Rosner, 'leisure handwork also focuses attention [on] the pleasures of hard work under the right circumstances.'

Not surprisingly, some makers point to the psychological boost to their sense of self. Ramona Barry, co-author of *The Craft Companion* (with Rebecca Jobson) and the public programs officer with Craft Victoria, similarly describes how the process and the products she makes influence her sense of self. Craft, she says, 'gives me a way to be proud of myself. In that respect it's the best friend I've ever had'.

More Than Value for Money

'It is striking to note,' writes psychologist Mihaly Csikszentmihalyi, 'how inexpensive things that stand for kinship and relatedness tend to be. Tokens of remembrance, respect, and love typically have trivial intrinsic value, and the labour invested in them is usually voluntary.' As I finished stitching the pieces of the rabbit body together, and pushed the scissor's blunt nose inside the fabric, I knew that the first gift had come together. As the jumble of loose threads and raw edges disappeared inside the torso, I knew the rabbits would work. First, one gangly arm emerged and then another, followed by one leg and the other. Success.

122

Finally, I knew why I was making. Why I was right to buy the grey flannel fabric a year earlier. Right in my longing to take this flat horizon and transform it into something. Right to make something that was truly mine, in order to give it away. As unlikely as they were, the rabbits represented afternoons and evenings stolen from an unwilling world, as American poet Thomas Faber describes writing—a reminder that much of what I am and value cannot find expression at a keyboard or at the checkout. Of course, buying a soft toy would have been quicker, easier and cheaper, but much less worth my while. The handmade object has a worth beyond the market, and it is, implicitly, a promise that we do as well.

The Empty Drawer

No account whatever had been taken of her relation to her treasures,
of the passion with which she had waited for them, worked for them,
picked them over, made them worthy of each other and the house,
watched them, loved them, lived with them.
Henry James, *The Spoils of Poynton*

The Gesture

The taxi was on its way.

'Let me show you these,' she says reaching into the drawer and pulling out a bundle of embroidered napkins, neatly tied together with string—this string I recognise from the brown paper parcels with beeswax she used to send across the seas.

'Isn't the handiwork wonderful?' she asks, drawing my attention to the embroidery of a distant relative. I feel I ought to know them by name, but I don't.

'Yes, wonderful.'

'Would you like them?'

'Oh, no, they are yours,' I answer, too quickly for politeness. 'I wouldn't appreciate them like you do. And you might need them.'

She leaves the room. I recheck the dodgy zip on my bulging backpack—will it last the distance home?

Next, she returns with a box, also tied up with string, that I've never seen before.

'I'd like to show you these boots. They're real Italian leather.'

Tan, long and decades old, still like new. She fell in love with them at first sight, she tells me, on seeing them in a shop window, and worked months to pay them off on lay-by. She used to look good in them. 'Very stylish,' she adds, and I try to imagine the hardworking woman of her youth.

'Do you like them?'

'Sure,' I shrug across the 60-year gap between us.

'Do you want them? Take them.'

Where had this come from? Confused, I am slow to grasp what is being asked of me, and why. A white-knuckle flyer at the best of times, my mind is preoccupied with the long flight ahead of me. And, after five weeks' carrying my life on my back, I don't want to lift another thing, let alone these high-heeled boots I could probably find in any op shop back home. I am about to say as much when she speaks again.

'Why don't you just try them on?'

The taxi hasn't yet arrived. I suppose I *could try*. I kick off my stinking sneakers and, comically, like one of Cinderella's sisters, stuff my feet into the petite size 6 boots. She beams—at seeing the boots, as much as at me—and I cannot refuse her gift, despite my bafflement about the gesture.

Fifteen years later I pull the boots from the bottom drawer of my wardrobe on the other side of the world.

The ambivalence and confusion come back. My nanna has now been dead for over ten years. I am no longer a young backpacker, but a middle-aged parent. The boots, however, are unchanged. They still look new. They even came back into fashion again in the year she died—I suspect this would've pleased her. But I've only worn them a few times. I've tried to make them mine, and failed. Not only are they too small, they're also 'not me'. And they never were. This is one of the strangest relationships I have with an object. I possess the boots, but they are not mine.

I am simply their custodian. For now. Why did she want me to have them? And why did I accept them? As I pack them away again, I realise I have never answered these questions.

In Life and Death

'Everyone knows the power of things,' writes philosopher Simone de Beauvoir in her account of her mother's death, *A Very Easy Death*, 'life is solidified in them, more immediately present than in any one of its instants.' Yet without the life that animates and gives objects meaning, their importance evaporates, de Beauvoir continues. They become 'orphaned, useless, waiting to turn into rubbish or to find another identity'. This is the conclusion many of us seek to avoid, especially for our most meaningful, beloved possessions.

Possessions have a curious relationship to life, death and loss. They are the props that support us in the almost invisible, often unconsidered task of being alive. They can, as de Beauvoir observes, give this fleeting life a solid form that we can look at and hold onto. The stable material world can anchor our continuity and, to an extent, compensate for the transience of human existence. As de Beauvoir observes in her study *Old Age*, 'the things that belong to us are as it were solidified habits—the mark of certain repetitive forms of appropriate behaviour ... this armchair is waiting for me to sit in it every evening'.

To have, own and use familiar things is such a crucial part of living that we devote considerable time, effort and money to them. As writer Dominique Browning argues recently in *The New York Times*, 'over the course of a lifetime, we forage, root and rummage around in our stuff, because that is what it means to be human'.

Yet, this dependence on our possessions is also a source of fear and disquiet. Even as these objects anchor us in daily life, their anchor might easily become a burdensome weight, if only psychologically. On some level, though, we know it is somewhat futile to cling to things that will become ephemeral with our death. 'Death,' as sociologist Margaret Gibson frankly puts it, 'makes all material possessions nomadic.' From mundane objects like bathplugs and brooms, to precious ones like wedding rings and children's drawings, the stuff of daily life will one day be untethered. As the Flemish still-life 'Vanitas' artists were at pains to point out in their paintings: no amount of beautiful possessions will change that each of us will die one day. Despite the pleasures and comforts we find in our possessions, these things will endure without us. Even much-adored boots.

The Weight of Things

It was not only the gift of the boots that caught me off my guard. It was also the lightness and ease with which my nanna gave something so personally significant. And to me, someone so reckless when it came to footwear—she had seen the state of my sneakers. Her ease contradicts popular beliefs about older people, such as the idea they unreasonably cling to their possessions, often alienating and angering their adult children in the process. It flies in the face of all the tales of pathological hoarding and grief at clearing the parental home, which seem to regularly fill the weekend magazines.

In this narrative of thing-stifled grief, possessions are actual or anticipated burdens that weigh on and worry us, expending our energy when it is in short supply. I don't doubt that this is true for some, especially where the potent mix of pathological hoarding, excessive clutter, grief or illness is concerned. Journalist Stephanie Wood, for example, recently described the labour-intensive sifting and sorting she undertook of her parents' large house—a home too full of several generations' worth of things. 'There can be no joy in this process,' she writes. 'A parent (or both) is dead or dying or in care. It is the end of something, never a beginning. In our case, my father is dead, my mother is grieving and I am angry.'

Wood acknowledges the bittersweet aspects of what she calls an 'exhumation'; the little discoveries she made about her family history and characters buried in the mountain of stuff left behind: in desks, cupboards, even under the house. Despite these unexpected rewards, the dominant feeling that runs through her account is guilty resentment. She resents the time-sucking futility of dealing with the sheer bulk of another's material load. And the clashes it brings with her grieving mother over trivial things, such as the glass jars her mother will not throw away and insists on washing for the op shop.

With healthier ageing, longer lives, and more material wealth all round, many of us can expect to know both sides of this coin. For some, such as Wood, this burden is faced or anxiously anticipated. This responsibility is part of what it means to have kin. We might hope it to be simple, smooth and easy, but it is unreasonable to expect that it will be.

But this is a one-sided picture of possessions in later life, or after death, which emphasises the losses, burdens and sadness, and overlooks its more positive counterparts: giving, lightening and hope. This is the quieter story of how some people come to terms with their mortality and, in doing so, transform their relationships with possessions. It is the narrative of preparing for a good death by letting go. It is not effacement, but the excitement, ease and relief I saw in my nanna when she knew I would take her boots.

Being Mortal

Contrary to common stories of burden and loss, some enter later life taking decisive action to gain control and find new homes for important objects before they die. This can occur as a slowly increasing awareness of mortal limits, or begin abruptly in response to a key life change, such as illness or injury. Anthropologists and sociologists give this process various names, such as divestment, inventory reduction, dispersal ritual and transmission project. 'Transmission project', coined by anthropologist Jean-Sébastien Marcoux, in particular speaks to the decisive shift in what is being done with the objects, as well as the scale and prolonged nature of the task—of the clearing, sorting and giving actions freely repeated by an individual over time.

My nanna's transmission project had no obvious trigger, no immediate necessity—or none that I was aware of. Her house was tiny, tidy and uncluttered, and she was a mobile, independent octogenarian in good health. She would continue to make the long journey halfway around the world to visit her family for several more years to come. There was no sense that she thought the end was nigh. Yet, in hindsight, the order of her home implied she was probably well into this 'project'. She also showed no hesitation in giving the boots away, suggesting she had already decided the time was right to separate from them.

This decisiveness and intensity of letting go seems to be marked with advancing age, but it is not a practice that is distinct to the elderly. Sociologist Anne Karpf, in *How to Age*, says that ageing well is a lifelong process, with certain dispositions needing to be practised throughout our lives. One of these practices, Karpf argues, is a preparedness to relinquish 'friends, old roles, even possessions that belonged to earlier stages of life ... at every stage of life some attachments need to be given up for others to develop, in order to move forward'.

Why, though, does the urge to let go or transfer objects suddenly take off in later life? Why bother with this springcleaning in the autumn of one's life?

Key thinkers in this area point to a heightened aware-ness of our own death as the trigger. We all know we'll die one day, but this is an abstract fact. Key life changes, such the deaths of friends, or advanced age, make this fact more vivid and unavoidable. Anthropologist Beverly Morris says that when we reach a 'death awareness threshold' it fundamentally transforms our relationship to the things we own. Morris proposes that once a person reaches their threshold, this knowledge pushes them into 'divesting' action. While this threshold might vary for each person, once reached, the subsequent action follows a common trajectory of sorting, throwing or giving away, and planning.

This mortal reckoning can clarify just how deeply some things matter, and how others fall away easily. Precious or 'cherished objects', as consumer behaviour scholar Russell Belk puts it, 'are experienced as extraordinary and emotion-provoking rather than as merely functional; owners of such treasured objects are generally unwilling to sell them for market value or otherwise dispose of them'. It is also to soberly consider what will become of these objects in a future without us.

The value they have for us, which is partly given by us, is unlikely to be sustained without our presence. 'It won't stay here,' said one older woman of disposing of her family treasures, in the study by sociologists Jonathan Marx, Jennifer Crew Solomon and Lee Q. Miller. 'It will disappear is what it boils down to.' If valued objects aren't placed in safe hands by us, they will be reduced to their crude market value: what others will pay to either buy them or dispose of them.

Things Left Behind

'There is nothing which is more surely part of yourselves,' writes historian of taste James Laver, 'than the decor of our lives.' Upon our death, this material legacy will tell a story of this self, and those facing death sometimes go to great lengths to shape this story. They might dispose of, even destroy, objects. Letters are burned, or only the best works of art or craft are kept. This might be because of an intense wish for privacy, but it also may be an active attempt to shape how we see ourselves in life, and how others see us after death. In getting rid of some things, we are choosing not to be associated with them, or a particular action. The author Henry James, for example, burned large numbers of personal letters he received during his lifetime, and asked others to do the same to the ones he wrote to them. He wrote to one correspondent: 'Burn my letter with fire or candle (if you have either! Otherwise, wade out into the sea with it and soak the ink out of it).'

Yet, this isn't an action only undertaken by the shy, famous or deeply narcissistic, but a trend observed among ordinary people approaching death. 'Before they die,' argues sociologist David Unruh, 'people interpret and apportion cues to their personal identities for those who will survive.' Similarly, anthropologist Beverly Morris contends 'that some individuals are so concerned with what their image will be after their death that the selection and distribution of personal possessions is an attempt at impression management'. This act is a strategic final attempt to gain the upper hand in shaping how we'll be remembered.

The Promise of Things

I don't yet understand what it feels like to get to an advanced age—to know for certain that more of my life is behind than in front of me. To make jokes, as my mother does, about only having 'another ten good years'. But I know what it feels like to be ill, weak, vulnerable. I have, more than once, heard the 'eternal footman' walking too closely behind my back for comfort. I now keenly feel my time is limited. And this experience starkly reshaped my attachments to objects, weakening many and strengthening those to a select few.

I was surprised how swiftly long-held assumptions were transformed. Returning home weak from hospital after sudden illness loosened my attachment to things that a few weeks earlier I'd thought were a necessary part of myself. The craft projects, for instance, I had waiting for time to complete, the oddments I'd collected just for the sake of having another curious thing, became questionable. A serious illness showed that the future was finite—there would not be time for all ambitions and experiences. And I realised that I did not want to be surrounded by the incompleteness of unrealised projects that I would probably never begin. These were an unfocused grab bag of unrealisable possibilities I'd greedily clung to.

But more than this, I saw my room as others would have seen it if I had died that night in the emergency room— it was now no longer an 'if', but a 'when' I die. On the day I returned, when I could barely walk to the end of my bed before my legs buckled, all I wanted to achieve was to sweep around and quickly put all these objects back to rights, but I couldn't even do this. Powerless, I saw the work my loved ones would have had to do to sort through it, and how they would've seen me as a result. As soon as I was well enough, I began to prune my things to better reflect myself in these objects, as much for myself as for others. I remain a thingly person, but more intentionally selective, critical and less burdened by stuff.

'Objects are not just things left behind,' argue ethnologists Lene Otto and Lykke L. Pedersen, who studied collections bequested to the Copenhagen Museum. These collections 'actively code memory and they "tell" a life story'. But this story can be more than the raw debris that is 'visible proof of a life lived'. It is an opportunity to preserve the better aspects of our self in the memories of the people we leave behind.

Breaking the House

The French have a phrase for it: 'Casser maison'. Literally it means 'breaking the house', but anthropologist Jean-Sébastien Marcoux extends the phrase to what people seek to do in that process. Beyond clearing, curation and memory-shaping comes the generosity of the final step: transmitting or gifting personal objects. Marcoux describes this as a 'matter of performing the inheritance before time, of preparing one's death'. Here begins the interpersonal task of finding another who shares common ground, perhaps only aesthetically.

Accepting an object, now or in advance, vindicates the owner's action and holds out the hope of them being remembered, even if this is not guaranteed. The giving of such objects, as Marcoux points out, is akin to a ritual sacrifice that expresses 'the desire for continuity: the desire to perpetuate oneself'. It is the hopeful gesture that something of us will endure, even though what we are perishes.

What might a successful transmission project look like? What becomes of this curated assemblage? What about the inheritors?

The ideal transfer of possessions might, to some, look like psychoanalyst Sigmund Freud's bequest to his daughter Anna. He left her the collection of antiquities in his study—his famous 'grubby gods'—and his library, including the now famous consulting couch. These objects had come with him to London from Vienna in 1938, when the Freud family fled the Nazi-occupied city. Freud was to die the following year.

But the objects did not become nomads. Anna became the protector of both his reputation and his things. Aside from giving some items to the Sigmund Freud Museum in Vienna, Anna preserved them all in his London home for over forty years, until she died in 1982, and the home became a museum. 'When in July 1986 Maresfield Gardens opened to the public as the Freud Museum, everything was just as Freud had left it,' writes Janine Burke in her biography *The Spinx on the Table*. 'The visitor's first impression is of a marvellous museum, quiet as a tomb.'

The preservation of Freud's object legacy is exceptional. It is the result of Anna's devotion to her father's reputation and her ability to keep his things intact. And the museum has ensured that this famous legacy endures—even the sagging and worn-out consulting couch restored through the Freud Museum's 2013 appeal to raise £5000. This, though, is no ordinary couch, but a cultural symbol of Freud's 'talking therapy'. Its historical and cultural value now far outweigh its material decay. As Dawn Kemp, the Freud Museum's acting director, puts it, it is 'possibly the most famous piece of furniture in the world'. Freud's fame has ensured not only the enduring value of his possessions, but also the maintenance of them as a collection.

But few adult children are in Anna Freud's position: able to give up their own space or willing to get rid of their own things in order to keep their parents' material legacy intact. Ordinary people's couches and ornaments, no matter how important they were in their lives, are usually ordinary and dispersed. And most are unlikely to maintain their significance when severed from their original owner.

Although some inheritors do keep rooms of bequeathed furniture, such an inheritance is often an ambivalent one. For instance, a woman who took part in Beverly Morris's study of divesting action declares that she was not a collector, despite living in a house full of antiques. 'I just was the only one left when everybody else moved on ... I felt if they were in the family I should take care of them.' But this was far from her own taste. 'No,' she reflects, 'if all this was destroyed and I started over, I'd get Swedish modern. I love it.'

Another barrier to the transmission project is finding a home for old objects in this time of material plenty. Tastes have changed and, while hand-me-downs and heirlooms once found grateful recipients, this is no longer the case. Relative affluence in most Western countries has granted a material freedom that now extends to even their poorest citizens. And with this material independence has come the rise of personal choice. We take it as given that we will be able to express ourselves through the things we choose to own, rather than having this decided for us by poverty or the accidents of inheritance. Further complicating the way that material objects have become a means of personal expression, as sociologists Jonathan Marx, Jennifer Crew Solomon and Lee Q. Miller point out, is the fact that they have also become increasingly disposable. Personal taste, which is easy prey to marketing, devalues both the old and inherited and the relatively new, creating considerable hurdles to passing things on. In the absence of shared understandings and value placed on objects, there is little to resist this trend of general disposability.

Gifts, as the French anthropologist Marcel Mauss famously argues, are never free of obligation, even if the only obligation implied is the onus to accept the gift. But the gift gesture can be refused for a variety of reasons to do with the relationship rather than the object. Some might refuse or reject gifted objects when they question the motive of those giving, the obligation it implies, or unstated assumptions about superior value. Writer Dominique Browning, for example, acknowledges that her sons' 'homes may be full of their own things', but still thinks they ought to take her objects:

> I have started saying things to my sons like: 'When I die, just please, rent a warehouse, and put everything away. You are too young to understand the value of what I have bought. Someday you will want these things, and you'll only have to shop in your own warehouse.'

These objects, and the memories they conjure, cannot be controlled. While Browning wants the reassurance of continued ties through her bequested objects—'I will be watching down on them from the walls and the shelves, having somehow transmogrified myself into my stuff'— objects can also haunt, restrict and dominate their care-takers. Gifting is not one way, but a dance that requires acceptance, often of more than just the gift. And inheri-tors might knowingly resist such attempts to shape their lives through such bequests. The objects we think of as wonderful might have different meanings to others. 'Some find the reminiscences haunting,' argues sociolo-gist David Unruh, 'while others revel in continued ties to the deceased.'

Even when differences of value, or rejection of kin-ship ties, are not a problem, even when others can see the value of a requested object, it isn't always possible to accept and keep it. Poet August Kleinzahler, in his moving account of clearing out his parents' home in the *London Review of Books*, describes the hidden torture of having to pull apart their material lives. He writes, 'the truth is that I was reluctant, viscerally, psychologically, to let any of it go'. His late father's collection of objects—'small stat-ues, figurines, odd bits of driftwood or stone he'd picked up'—were still there as his mother moved into care. To Kleinzahler they were more than just dreadful knick-knacks, as the real estate agents saw them. They 'were all lovely, all interesting; he had a wonderful eye. But they were of no value to anyone else, except perhaps to me, and I don't have room.' Faced with limited time to empty the house, he ended up putting them in the bin.

Even with the best of plans, without what sociologist David Ekerdt calls 'acts of reception', the giving gesture hangs empty in the air. No matter how beautiful, rare or loved our things are by us, we might try to place them in vain. She 'hoped that those things would interest someone because these mattered to her', writes Marcoux of the unsuccessful transmission project of one of the elderly people in his study. 'But nobody came to choose them. No one responded to her invitation.' When no one wants your things, irrespective of their reasons, when you cannot sell them or even give them away, the transmission project is unexpectedly halted. There is no affirmation of self or relationships, no affirmation of the life lived and poured into objects. It can be lonely when no one wants your things, especially those that were most admired and enjoyed. The failure of the transmission exposes a fundamental aloneness we can usually deny. An inability to safely place your things, as Marcoux puts it, 'forces one to take the measure of one's isolation'.

Fundamentally, another cannot experience and appreciate our precious things as we do. They are ours alone. Crucial, then, to the process of letting go of a precious, beloved object seems to be acknowledging the limits of their importance for us and for others. Some researchers advise a tough-love exposing of this fact, alongside practical strategies to articulate, convey and create shared meanings. Jonathan Marx and colleagues argue, 'do not blindly assume that relatives share their attachments to objects. An essential element in the successful transfer of an object is that the receivers understand the significance of the object to the giver and/or to family history.'

Realistic preparations that take this into account might help secure a home for objects despite considerable impediments to their acceptance. Actively preparing meaningful objects for transmission seems to help. Some people label objects, for instance, naming who they are intended for and providing a note of their personal importance or the story that goes with them. 'This was done by actually placing labels on the item, marking the item in some way, writing the information down elsewhere or by transmitting this information verbally,' observes Beverly Morris. Storytelling also seems to help the owner to relinquish the object. Some people continue to live with these things, even after they have made decisions about who they will eventually go to.

Reason's Limits

'As she undid the black ribbon', Simone de Beauvoir's sister Poupette 'began to cry'. In the shadow of their mother's death, even her ordinary possessions took on a new significance. 'It's so stupid,' says Poupette, 'and I'm not at all a worshipper of things, but I can't throw this ribbon away.' Simone advises, unexpectedly, to keep the ribbon before addressing us, the readers, with the following advice: 'It is useless to try to integrate life and death and to behave rationally in the presence of something that is not rational: each must manage as well as he can in the tumult of his feelings'.

Transmission projects are precisely this: reasonable efforts to take responsibility for the muddle of things we acquire over a lifetime. Passing these on is a modest expression of optimism that something will remain after we've gone. Placing our objects with others is an expression of hope in a future without us. Too much focus on the objects themselves, however, overlooks what the transmission ritual, ultimately, achieves for the individual. If possessions help us to create stable meaning in our lives, then transmission helps prepare us for a good death—one in which we have some degree of control over our possessions, even if our own matter will eventually evade our control. The chief shift, as Marcoux puts it, is that 'it is the transmission project in itself rather than the collection of things as a collection that embodies the donor's selfhood and the potential realization for the self'. We become more ourselves in the sacrifice of giving.

My English nanna—a true cockney, as she would proudly proclaim to anyone who mistook her for a common Londoner—would've turned 100 this week. Like many of her generation, her most prized possession was a small collection of fine jewellery, commemorating birthdays and anniversaries, but some rings and brooches were stolen in a break-in one evening, during the desperate Thatcher years, as she and my grandfather sat watching television in the adjoining room. She grieved this loss, but in many ways the boots were more representative of who she was: independent, hardworking, with a dash of her own suntanned style. Along with a chunky ceramic bracelet and a handful of blue lettergrams, they are the only tangible links I now have to her. Each time I unpack them, they bring with them the lost world in which she sent her distinctive blue lettergrams, which arrived by plane and talked about the English weather. They prompt a mix of memories, happiness and sadness. But then my young daughter puts an enthusiastic claim on the boots, as she has done on half the clothes in my wardrobe, and I am back in this world and her future. And I reflect that my 7-year-old's uncomplicated verve for these boots would make my nanna very happy.

Foucault's Toolbox

'I would like my books to be a kind of tool-box which others can rummage through to find a tool which they can use however they wish in their own area,' writes the French philosopher Michel Foucault in a 1974 essay. Foucault wanted his work to be 'useful'. 'I don't write for an audience,' he adds, 'I write for users, not readers.' While some might disagree about the utility of his work, which can be difficult to grasp, his intention is one that I endorse. And to that end, I share the books, essays and articles that have formed my toolbox.

But, like any toolbox, it depends on the ends to which you put these means. None of the works described here, with the notable exception of Marie Kondo's guidebooks, are manuals for action. Instead, they are ideas for thinking about what an intelligent life with things might entail. As essayist Rebecca Solnit suggests in her book *Encyclopedia of Trouble and Spaciousness* (Trinity University Press, San Antonio), they might be 'both a bundle of ideas and another twig to lay on the future fire of your home'. Some ideas are consoling, others incendiary.

It is in this spirit of cautious ambivalence that I share the 'idea bundles' that have shaped, goaded, inspired and challenged me while writing *The Promise of Things*. None promise you a pristine cupboard of bleached white towels, perfectly folded fitted sheets, or the magic to keep time still. My view is that life with objects requires thought and reflection, and it is not a state we attain once and for all. Rather, it is a life we muddle towards and keep muddling within constraints not of our own choosing: financial, familial, economic and social expectation.

The tools described here range from academic essays, written chiefly for other academics and specialised debates (many of the authors, to my surprise, are sociologists) to the regular, accessible analyses found in weekend newspapers. Many explore the vexed problems posed by how material plenitude and globalised culture impinge on our lives, often in new and uncomfortable ways. Some are books I own or come from university libraries, but a vast number come from the shared resource that is the local public library.

In addition to these tools, I've also listed a few extra titles that you will not find on any of this book's pages: poems about bicycles, disappointment and bones; a book about people, houses and memory—all written by poets. In a few well-chosen words, the poet's tools cut to the core of an argument, experience or anxiety—read them if you dare.

Epigraph

The book's first epigraph is writer Gerald Brenan's dismissal of Dora Carrington as a serious artist because, in his view, she lacked the essential focus to make art. Brenan's letter is quoted in Virginia Nicholson's *Among the Bohemians: Experiments in Living 1900–1939* (Harper Collins, New York, 2002, p. 212). Carrington's love of mismatched, old and curious 'junk' is further described by Nicholson in the chapter 'Dwelling with Beauty'. 'I selected 5 exquisite old coffee cups, of finest china, with saucers, all sprigged and different,' Carrington is quoted by Nicholson as saying of her recent junk-shop finds. 'Three without handles.'

143

Matisse's Armchair

Matisse's attachment to particular possessions, and their role in his art while at the Villa le Rêve, during and after World War II, is explored by Marie-France Boyer in the beautiful *Matisse at Villa le Rêve* (Thames & Hudson, London). This glossy little book includes black-and-white photographs by Hélène Adant of the artist at work, his objects, and the house and garden, as well as excerpts of Matisse's letters to Louis Aragon. Aragon's quip about Matisse's character-filled armchairs is reported in Jo Anna Isaak's *Feminism and Contemporary Art* (Routledge, London).

Matisse's post-illness life is discussed in Alastair Sooke's concise and insightful *Henri Matisse: A Second Life* (Penguin, London), which explores the post-illness creativity in Matisse's final years. It reveals Matisse as a man racing against time to bring his project to his own artistic 'conclusion'. Matisse's late feeling for life, and the vital energetic force and commitment behind his artistic project, is also described in T.J. Clark's essay 'The Urge to Strangle' in the 5 June 2014 issue of the *London Review of Books*.

A few of Matisse's own brief writings on art, drawing and painting appear in Herschel B. Chipp's *Theories of Modern Art* (University of California Press, Berkeley).

Hilary Spurling's two-volume biography provides the longer perspective on Matisse's life and its influences, including the link between Matisse's family history as weavers—his great-grandfather was a linen weaver—and his aesthetic eye, his love of fabrics and textiles, and his stubborn attachment to everyday luxury. The early years of Matisse's life from 1869 to 1908 are covered in Spurling's *The Unknown Matisse* (Alfred A. Knopf, New York), while *Matisse, The Master* (Hamish Hamilton, London), covers 1909 until his death in 1954.

My edition of writer Georges Perec's first novel, *Things: A Story of the Sixties* (Harvill, Hammersmith), is published in an edition with another of his stories, *A Man Asleep*. *Things* was first published in France in 1965 as *Les Choses* (Editions Julliard).

George Monbiot's column 'Materialism: A System That Eats Us from the Inside Out' was published in *The Guardian* (9 December 2013).

Psychologist Mihaly Csikszentmihalyi's essay 'Why We Need Things' is an accessible introduction to key ideas in his work on objects. It is published as part of a collection of essays: *History from Things: Essays on Material Culture*

(Smithsonian Books, Washington) edited by Stevan Lubar and W. David Kingery.

Marsha Richins and colleagues' work on materialism is published in a succession of academic research articles in consumer research and marketing journals. They include Richins and Peter H. Bloch's 1986 paper, 'After the New Wears Off: The Temporal Context of Product Involvement', in volume 13 of the *Journal of Consumer Research*. Published in volume 40 of the same journal is Richins' 2012 paper, 'When Wanting is Better than Having: Materialism, Transformation Expectations, and Product-Evoked Emotions in the Purchase Process'. Richins published another paper with Peter H. Bloch, 'Post-Purchase Product Satisfaction: Incorporating the Effects of Involvement and Time', in 1991 in volume 23 of the *Journal of Business Research*. Richins' paper with colleagues Kim K.R. McKeage and Debbie Najjar, 'An Exploration of Materialism and Consumption-Related Affect' was published in 1992 in volume 19 of the journal *Advances in Consumer Research*. Richins' paper 'Materialism, Transformation Expectations, and Spending: Implications for Credit Use' was published in volume 30 of the 2011 *Journal of Public Policy & Marketing*.

An accessible introduction to the psychology of materialism is Tim Kasser's *The High Price of Materialism* (MIT Press, Cambridge).

Artist Michael Landy's *Break Down* can be found on YouTube, alongside documentaries about him and his art performance. His conversation with art historian and curator Julian Stallabrass is published online at Artangel (artangel.org.uk). Art critic Sebastian Smee's essay on

Landy's performance art, 'Ghost in the Machine', appeared in *The Australian* newspaper on 21 August 2007. Andrew O'Hagan's essay 'The Things We Throw Away' is from the May 24 2007 *London Review of Books*. Landy was interviewed nine years after *Break Down* by Lena Corner in the 2010 *Independent* article 'Has Destroying All Their Worldly Goods Made These Artists Happy?'

If you haven't heard, Marie Kondo's bestselling books are called *The Life-Changing Magic of Tidying Up: The Japanese Art of Decluttering and Organizing* (Ten Speed Press, Berkeley) and *Spark Joy: An Illustrated Guide to The Japanese Art of Tidying* (Ebury, London). Kondo's guidebook has inspired numerous essays and opinion pieces in praise of its effectiveness.

The reflective or critical pieces I've drawn on are fewer. Susan Bolotin's comments appear in the 2015 *Wall Street Journal* article 'Marie Kondo and the Cult of Tidying Up'.

Psychoanalyst Christopher Bollas writes about the relationship between affect, feeling and emotion in *The Evocative Object World* (Routledge, London).

Adele Chapin's reflection on decluttering Kondo-style, 'Will Tidying Guru Marie Kondo's Cleaning Advice Really Change Your Life?', is online at www.racked.com.

Csikszentmihalyi and Eugene Rochberg-Halton's rich, fascinating and comprehensive research on people and their special objects was published as *The Meaning of Things* (Cambridge University Press, Cambridge) in 1981.

Juliet Schor's essay 'Learning Diderot's Lesson: Stopping the Upward Creep of Desire' is published in a collection of essays edited by Tim Jackson, *Sustainable Consumption* (Routledge, London).

Laura Miller's essay 'Someday Never Comes' was published in *The Slate Book Review*.

Clive Hamilton and Richard Denniss's discussion of the extent and impact of contemporary material aspirations is published as *Affluenza: When Too Much is Never Enough* (Allen & Unwin, Crows Nest). James Twitchell's case for understanding the allure of materialism is from *Lead Us Into Temptation: The Triumph of American Materialism* (Columbia University Press, New York).

Philosopher Crispin Sartwell and essayist Rebecca Solnit are two of my favourite writers and thinkers. Sartwell's meditation on the need for resetting experience is from *The Six Names of Beauty* (Routledge, London), while Solnit's distinction between materialism and deep attention to materials is from her brilliant essay 'Inside Out, or Interior Space (and Interior Decoration)' in the *Encyclopedia of Trouble and Spaciousness* (Trinity University Press, San Antonio).

147

The Edwardian Wardrobe

The introductory quotation about wardrobes is from French philosopher Gaston Bachelard's exploration of domestic spaces and experiences in *The Poetics of Space* (Beacon Press, Boston).

The statistics on the number of clothes women owned in 1930s America come from Emma Johnson's article in *Forbes*, 'The Real Cost of Your Shopping Habits', 15 January 2015. The statistics for Britain come from *Stuffocation* author James Wallman's January 24 2015 article 'Viewpoint: The Hazards of Too Much Stuff' for the BBC Online.

Sociologists Tony Kearon and Rebecca Leach's ideas about the 'habitus of comfort' in which objects lose their 'thingliness' is from their academic essay 'Invasion of the 'Body Snatchers': Burglary Reconsidered' in the journal *Theoretical Criminology* (4/4, 2000).

Gerontologist David J. Ekerdt's excellent and clarifying essay 'Dispossession: The Tenacity of Things' is published as part of an edited academic collection called *Consumption and Generational Change: The Rise of Consumer Lifestyles* (Transaction Publishers, New Brunswick).

William Morris's ideas about home interiors, beauty and society are widely quoted in books and on the Internet, but rarely read in their wider context as public talks. 'The Beauty of Life', with its famous prescriptions about simplicity, beauty and utility, was delivered to the Birmingham Society of Arts and School of Design in 1880. It is clear, straightforward and, along with his strong words for the pollution industry, remains relevant today. I found it in a small 1919 collection of Morris's talks entitled *Hopes and Fears for Art* (Longmans, Green and Co. New York).

David Lowenthal's epic *The Past is a Foreign Country* is published by Cambridge University Press, London.

Artist Vanessa Bell's 1960 letter to her daughter Angelica is quoted in Frances Spalding's biography *Vanessa Bell* (Tempus, Stroud). Her sister Virginia Woolf once confided a similar remark to her diary, 'What a curious sense the clothes sense is!', after a shopping trip with Angelica, her niece, on 23 January 1935. Her diary is lightly sprinkled with such observations.

Psychologist Barry Schwartz's *The Paradox of Choice: Why Less is More* (ECCO, New York) is an accessible discussion of why more choice can be a burden, as well as strategies to make good-enough decisions.

In addition to being an accessible, expansive discussion of beauty, philosopher Crispin Sartwell's *Six Names of Beauty* (Routledge, London) is itself a beautiful-looking book.

The work of Australian artist Grace Cossington Smith is in many Australian art galleries. Her 1955 *Interior with Wardrobe Mirror* is in the collection of the Art Gallery of New South Wales. Several sketches of her Turramurra bedroom can be seen in Daniel Thomas's *Grace Cossington Smith: A Life* (The National Gallery of Australia, Canberra). A variety of her work is available online through state gallery websites.

Sam Gosling's *Snoop: What Your Stuff Says About You* (Basic Books, New York) is an accessible discussion of people, personality and possessions. Daniel Kahneman's work with colleagues on 'peak-end' experience is discussed in his *Thinking, Fast and Slow* (Farrar, Straus & Giroux, New York.)

The Ithaka Stone

I recommend Yannis Ritsos's suite of poems—'Departures I', 'II', and 'III'—which are ostensibly about leaving, but evoke the feeling of life being emptied out. They are published in *Yannis Ritsos: Selected Poems, 1936–1988* (Boa Editions, Brockport).

Architect and essayist Witold Rybczynski's *Home: A Short History of an Idea* (Viking, New York) is one of those striking books that is not as well known as it ought to be. I found it in my local public library, as I did

Frank R. Wilson's *The Hand* (Vintage, New York) and John M. Henshaw's *A Tour of the Senses* (John Hopkins Press, Baltimore).

Sociologist Tim Dant's academic book *Material Culture in the Social World* (Open University Press, Milton Keynes) is an accessible discussion on thoughts and debates, as is fellow sociologist Deborah Lupton's paper 'Infants and/as objects' hosted on academia.edu.

Maurice Merleau-Ponty's radio lectures on embodiment are published as an attractive small book, *The World of Perception* (Routledge, London).

I bought my copy of Thalma Lobel's bestseller *Sensation: The New Science of Physical Intelligence* (Scribe, Melbourne) on the recommendation of Melbourne's Embiggen Books owner Warren Bonnet.

Richard Louv's *Last Child in the Woods* (Atlantic, London) came from the local library, as did Oliver Sacks' *An Anthropologist on Mars* (Picador, London)—as our copy of Sacks has gone missing (but, I hope, being read).

Deborah Needleman's friendly and beautiful hardback *The Perfectly Imperfect Home* (Clarkson Potter, New York) features pretty watercolour sketches of interiors.

Finally, my hardbound copy of Nikos Kazantzakis's *Report to Greco* (trans. P.A. Bien, Simon & Schuster, New York) was found in a junkshop in Tasmania's Beauty Point, near the Tamar River.

The Poäng

This chapter begins with a quotation from ceramic artist Edmund de Waal's *The White Road*, which describes his journeys in search of the origin stories of porcelain (Chatto & Windus, London).

Writer Meghan Daum's autobiography *Life Would Be Perfect If I Lived in That House* (Alfred A. Knopf, New York) is an entertaining self-examination of the role of wishing, hope and houses. Her account of living with provisional furniture is particularly insightful.

Anthropologist Janet Hoskins's essay 'Agency, Biography and Objects' is available online from academia.edu.

French sociologist Jean Baudrillard's 1968 book *The System of Objects* (Verso, London), according to Wikipedia, began as his doctoral thesis, 'Le Système des Objets (The System of Objects)'. It was completed under the supervision of the big names in twentieth-century theory: a 'dissertation committee of Henri Lefebvre, Roland Barthes, and Pierre Bourdieu'.

Architectural historian Steven Parissien's *Interiors: The Home Since 1700* (Laurence King Publishing, London) provides an accessible introduction and over-view of the trends and debates surrounding interiors, illustrated with colour photographs and advertising from various periods.

Deyan Sudjic, director of London's Design Museum, is the author of *The Language of Things* (Allen Lane, London), in addition to public talks and his accessible design commentary for *The Guardian* newspaper. His April 2006 review of Christopher Wilk's modernism exhibition at the V & A museum, 'Back to the Shiny New Future', and his article 'Is Modernism Dangerous?' were both published in *The Guardian*.

Foucault's Toolbox

Ellen Ruppel Shell's *Cheap: The High Cost of Discount Culture* (Penguin, New York) and *The New Yorker* writer Lauren Collins's article 'House Perfect? Is the IKEA Ethos Comfy or Creepy?' both explore the consequences of an addiction to quick, cheap fixes.

In his interview in bombmagazine.org with journalist Sameer Padania, psychoanalyst Adam Phillips explores the idea of an excess of information and suggestively describes capitalist culture as 'force-feeding us whether we're hungry or not. What this means is that we never know when we're hungry, and we don't have the space to figure out what it is we want.'

Csikszentmihalyi and Eugene Rochberg-Halton's research on people and special objects was published in *The Meaning of Things* (Cambridge University Press, Cambridge) in 1981.

Sociologist Zygmunt Bauman's *Liquid Times: Living in an Age of Uncertainty* (Polity, Cambridge) is not only an excellent introduction to his crucial perspective on modernity's shift from solid to liquid, but is also particularly insightful on the limits of the state in globalised culture, and how 'excess humans' are produced and treated. His chapter 'Humanity on the Move' is an important contribution to understanding the 'refugee problem'. And from the world's poorest to one of the richest: journalist Luke Harding's *Guardian* article '1974 IKEA chair, one careful owner, not for sale' (20 December 2006) describes Ikea's founder Ingvar Kamprad's enduring ownership and use of one of the first Poäng chairs his company produced. 'Mr Kamprad said he was very fond of his Japanese-designed Poäng chair and saw no reason why he should replace it.'

The Velvet Jacket

On promise and disappointment, I recommend Philip Larkin's 1951 poem 'Next, Please'. It was published in the 2003 edition of his *Collected Poems* (Faber and Faber, London).

Anthropologist Grant McCracken's ideas on how objects evoke our future selves are described in 'The Evocative Power of Things: Consumer Goods and the Preservation of Hopes and Ideals' in the collection edited by Tim Jackson, *Sustainable Consumption* (Routledge, London). Writer Rebecca Solnit's essay 'Inside Out, or Interior Space (and Interior Decoration)' appears in the collection of her essays, *Encyclopedia of Trouble and Spaciousness* (Trinity University Press, San Antonio).

John Carroll's book *Ego and Soul* is published by Counterpoint, Berkeley. Philosopher Susan Neiman's 2014 exploration of what maturity means is *Why Grow Up?* (Penguin, London).

On clothing, writer Jenny Diski's essay on its personal meaning for her appeared in the *London Review of Books* 'Diary' on 14 November 2002. Alexander Nagel's thoughts on style are in an interview in *Women in Clothes* (Penguin, London) by Sheila Heti, Heidi Julavits, Leanne Shapton and 639 others. D.W. Winnicott's unfinished 1964 talk 'The Concept of the False Self' is published in a collection of his essays, *Home is Where We Start From* (Penguin, London).

Anthropologist Janet Hoskins's essay 'Agency, Biography and Objects' is available online from academia.edu. Virginia Woolf's *Orlando* (Triad/Panther, St Albans) is easily found in paperback and in libraries, and, I imagine, ebooks. Her grand-niece Virginia Nicholson's book on those who live outside the mainstream is *Among the Bohemians* (Viking, London).

Simone de Beauvoir's Bicycle

I came across Michael Donaghy's poem 'Machines', describing the to and fro between rider and machine, while researching cycling experiences. It originally appeared in the September 1988 edition of Poetry magazine.

In Simone de Beauvoir's *Wartime Diary* (trans. Anne Deing Cordero; ed. Margaret A. Simons and Sylvie Le Bon de Beauvoir; University of Illinois, Urbana) she describes her early cycling experiences. Deirdre Bair's biography *Simone de Beauvoir: A Biography* (Vintage, London) provides the broader context for the wartime diary and letters. De Beauvoir's *The Blood of Others* (trans. Roger Senhouse and Yvonne Moyse; Pantheon Books, New York) was one of the first fiction books I read as a young adult. I was sentimentally attached to my pale-green-spine Penguin edition with a black-and-white photograph on the cover, but it has long been lost. My current Pantheon edition came into my possession courtesy of reviewer and writer James Tierney.

David V. Herlihy's *Bicycle: The History* (Yale University Press, New Haven) and Robert Penn's *It's All About the Bike: The Pursuit of Happiness on Two Wheels* (Penguin, London) were both borrowed from my local library.

On the definition of property, Lewis Hyde's summary features in *The Gift: Creativity and the Artist in the Modern World* (Vintage Books, New York), while

Margaret Radin's *Reinterpreting Property* (University of Chicago Press, Chicago) provides the chapter epigraph as well as the account of Hegel's *Philosophy of Right*.

Stanley Abercrombie's essay is the introduction to what appears to be a glossy industry publication, *Work, Life, Tools: The Things We Use to Do the Things We Do* (The Monocelli Press and Steel Case Design Partnership, New York). My husband, Damon Young, found it long ago and thought that I might find it useful, sooner or later.

Sociologist Tim Dant's account of the interplay between object and person is found in an unpublished paper, 'Playing with Things: Objects and Subjects in Windsurfing'.

Psychologist Mihaly Csikszentmihalyi's work on the concept of 'flow' was first published as an academic text, *Beyond Boredom and Anxiety* (Indiana University Press, Bloomington), and over a decade later as the popular *Flow* (Harper Collins, New York).

Sociologist Roger Caillois's account of play is from *Man, Play and Games* (trans. Meyer Barash; University of Illinois Press, Urbana), while the changing nature of leisure is described in Witold Rybczynski's August 1991 *The Atlantic* essay, 'Waiting for the Weekend'.

The Singer Sewing Machine

Philosopher Matthew Crawford's description of what distinguishes the craftsman from the consumer is from his book, *Shop Class as Soulcraft: An Inquiry Into the Value of Work* (Penguin, New York).

Faith Popcorn is a trendcaster. Her description of our hunger for 'human hands' is widely quoted, including by Stephanie Pearl-McPhee in her article 'The Knitting Revolution' on Craft Victoria's website.

Statistics on the uptake of craft and craft consumption are available in the reports of the Crafts Council of England, as well as the Australian Bureau of Statistics (4921.0 Participation in Selected Cultural Activities). Further analysis of participation and funding to support participation is provided in Ben Eltham's 2 March 2012 article for *Crikey* online, 'We Love Getting Crafty, But There's No Money in the Kitty'.

Sociologist Richard Sennett's *The Craftsman* (Penguin, London) is a rewarding book on the intertwining of the craftsman with her craft, including an accessible discussion of the 10 000-hour rule.

Senior curator of decorative arts and design at the National Gallery of Australia Robert Bell's *Material Culture: Aspects of Contemporary Australian Craft and Design* (National Gallery of Australia, Canberra) describes how artists and craftspeople tend to resist many of the pressures of globalisation, particularly the devaluation of materials.

Philosopher Karl Marx's idea about the relationship between the worker and the things he or she makes under a capitalist system is described in *Economic and Philosophic Manuscripts of 1844* (edited and with an introduction by Dirk J. Struik; International Publishers, United States).

The extent of China as the powerhouse of manufacturing is starkly illustrated by journalist Matt Schiavenza's article and accompanying infographic in *The Atlantic*, 5 August 2013, 'China's Dominance in Manufacturing— In One Chart'. Isobel Hilton's personal reflections on

China pre- and post-globalisation, 'Made in China', is in *Granta* 89, Spring 2005. This themed issue, 'The Factory', rewards wider reading, especially Desmond Barry's 'A Job on the Line', lest we fall prey to twee nostalgia about labour conditions closer to home.

Environmental writer Tanya Ha's personal reflection on how her favourite clothing is produced first appeared on Twitter. It is reprinted here with her permission.

Geographer David Harvey's *The Condition of Postmodernity* (Blackwell, Oxford) is, along with Bauman's work, crucial to understanding the consequences of and responses to globalised capitalism, particularly part III, 'The Experience of Space and Time'.

Marketing academics Christopher Fuchs, Martin Schreier and Stijn M.J. van Osselaer's article on the handmade effect, 'The Handmade Effect: What's Love Got to Do with It?', was published in the *Journal of Marketing* (volume 79, March 2015).

Publisher Geoff Slattery is quoted in the 2006 edition of *Handmade in Melbourne* (Geoff Slattery Publishing, Docklands) by Jan Phyland and Janet De Sliva. In a similar vein, including non-professional perspectives, is Faythe Levine and Cortney Heimerl's *Handmade Nation: The Rise of DIY, Art, Craft and Design* (Princeton Architectural, New York). Sociologist Betty Greer's essay on craft and labour is published in Levine and Heimerl's book.

Om Malik's 2013 interview with Etsy CEO Chad Dickerson about the online marketplace, 'Meet the Man Behind New York's Other Billion Dollar Internet Company. This One Makes Money' can be read online at gigaom.com. Nicole Vanderbilt's response to the changes in Etsy's definition of 'handmade' is quoted in *Mollie*

Makes magazine. These changes are also criticised in Grace Dobush's 'How Etsy Alienated Its Crafters and Lost its Soul' (19 February 2015) on wired.com.

Sociologist Colin Campbell's article 'The Craft Consumer' is from the academic journal *Journal of Consumer Culture* (volume 5(1), 2005), while Elizabeth Goodman and Daniela K. Rosner's research findings are published as 'From Garments to Gardens: Negotiating Material Relationships Online and "By Hand"' from *CHI 2011* (May 7–12 2011).

Crafter Ramona Barry was interviewed about the book she wrote with Rebecca Jobson, *The Craft Companion* (Thames & Hudson, Port Melbourne), in *The Age* newspaper (6 November 2015) by Frances Atkinson.

Finally, psychologist Mihaly Csikszentmihalyi's reminder that often the things we most value have little monetary worth is from his essay 'Why We Need Things' published in *History from Things: Essays on Material Culture* (Smithsonian Books, Washington) edited by Steven Lubar and W. David Kingery.

The Empty Drawer

This chapter begins with Henry James's tale of widowed Mrs Gereth's loss of her home and its contents with the marriage of her son, *The Spoils of Poynton* (Macmillan & Co, London). I also recommend poet Lisa Gorton's collection *Hotel Hyperion* (Giramondo, Artarmon), on lost things, place and memory, as well as her novel *The Life of Houses* (also Giramondo, Artarmon).

Philosopher Simone de Beauvoir wrote an extensive sociological and philosophical account of ageing (trans.

Patrick O'Brian; Penguin, London) as well as a moving personal account of her mother's death, *A Very Easy Death* (trans. Patrick O'Brian; Penguin, London).

Sociologist Margaret Gibson offers a more recent account of the role objects play in grief in *Objects of the Dead: Mourning and Memory in Everyday Life* (Melbourne University Press, Carlton).

Ageing and possessions is, increasingly, a topic of interest for academics, columnists and journalists. Journalist Stephanie Wood's personal account of helping her ageing mother clear her home, 'Home Truths', was published in Fairfax newspapers, 2 May 2015. Columnist Dominique Browning presents an opposing account in 'Let's Celebrate the Art of Clutter' (29 May 2015) in *The New York Times*. Sociologist and journalist Anne Karpf's *How to Age* (Pan Macmillan, London), in the accessible The School of Life series, discusses the mental work of ageing.

Academic works on ageing and possessions typically report observations based on what people actually do with their objects as they age. Anthropologist Jean-Sébastien Marcoux's empirical and theory-building account of the divesting rituals of elderly people in Montreal, 'The "Casser Maison" Ritual: Constructing the Self by Emptying the Home', was published in the *Journal of Material Culture* (1 July 2001). It is academic in tone, but is a very moving account of attempts to, and limits on, efforts to give things away. Anthropologist Beverly R. Morris's exploratory research on elderly women's divesting practices is from 'Reducing Inventory: Divestiture of Personal Possessions' in *Journal of Women & Aging* (volume 4 (2), 1992). Russell Belk's work on cherished objects is from 'Possessions and the Extended Self', *Journal of Consumer Research* (volume 15(2), 1988). Sociologists Jonathan I. Marx, Jennifer Crew Solomon and Lee Q. Miller's 'Gift Wrapping Ourselves: The Final Gift Exchange' is from the *Journal of Gerontology* (volume 59B, 2004). Sociologist David R. Unruh's paper 'Death and Personal History: Strategies of Identity Preservation' was published in *Social Problems* (volume 30(3), 1983).

Fashion historian James Laver's ideas about taste appear in his 1935 book *Taste and Fashion* (George G. Harrap & Company, London).

The anecdote about Henry James's diligent letter disposal is from Colm Tóibín's 'A Man with My Trouble' in the *London Review of Books*, 3 January 2008. Ethnologists Lene Otto and Lykke L. Pedersen's analysis of the personal collections left to the Copenhagen Museum makes for fascinating, goading reading. (*What kind of collector are you?* I asked myself as I read Otto and Pedersen's categories.) The article was published in 1998 as 'Collecting Oneself: Life Stories and Objects of Memory', in the journal for Nordic ethnology, *Ethnologia Scandinavica* (28).

Janine Burke's *The Sphinx on the Table* (Walker & Company, New York) describes a visit to the Freud Museum; while the museum's fundraising to restore Freud's couch is from Maev Kennedy's *Guardian* (6 May 2013) article, 'Interpretation of Seams? Sigmund Freud's Couch Needs £5,000 Restoration'.

Anthropologist Marcel Mauss's *The Gift* was published in a recent edition (Routledge, London).

Poet August Kleinzahler's 'Diary' account of clearing his parents' home in the *London Review of Books*

(11 February 2010) describes his grief at being unable to accept the wonderful things they had accumulated over their lifetime.

Finally, sociologist David J. Ekerdt offers, with Lindsey A. Baker, an account of 'The Material Convoy After Age 50' in the *Journals of Gerontology* (17 February 2015) and, with Aislinn Addington and Ben Hayter, 'Distributing Possessions: Personal Property Can Become a Social Matter' in *Generations* (volume 35[3], 2011).

Acknowledgements

Several years ago, fresh out of hospital, I wrote to make sense of my experience. I emailed the piece cold to an unknown editor of the weekend newspaper. That editor was Sally Heath. To my lasting surprise, Sally not only published that essay, but later commissioned this book. I owe her a great deal for her guidance, expertise and enthusiasm. My thanks extend to Melbourne University Press for supporting a first book by an emerging writer.

I was very fortunate to have three first readers of the manuscript. Damon Young, Matthew Lamb and Maureen Quibell each took the time to carefully read and critique the book, and encourage me to complete it. The book is vastly improved by their having read it. Any problems and limitations are, of course, mine.

My thanks are also due to copyeditor Meaghan Amor, who patiently and deftly dealt with missing words, scrambled sentences and my grammatical bugbears.

I was lucky to have the support of several literary organisations, directly or indirectly, at different stages of writing. I received assistance from the Melbourne Engagement Lab at the University of Melbourne in the book's formative stage. Without this formal recognition from the lab's director, Simon Clews, and its committee it is unlikely that I would've had the confidence to attempt the task. I am particularly grateful for the opportunity of

Acknowledgements

being regularly published in *Island* and *Womankind* magazines. These publications provided the essential grounding in writing for diverse audiences, and also helped pay the bills in order to keep writing.

Practically speaking, it was my husband, Damon, my mother, Maureen, and my mother-in-law, Allana, who provided many days of child-free writing time, especially during school holidays. For this, I am incredibly grateful.

I'd like to thank my children, Nikos and Sophia, who were not only patient with a distracted or absent mother throughout 2015, but also showed such care toward and excitement about the idea of the book.

And, finally, thank you to Damon for his enduring care and kindness. Without those emergency cups of tea, late-night chats, and the unbidden supply of white Lindt chocolate, this book would never have arrived.